The StrataPlay Methodology

Ludic Scholarship

Edited by Dr. Mila Zhu

Vol. 2

Mila Zhu

The StrataPlay Methodology

A Lorekeeper's Game Design in
Postqualitative Inquiry

New York · Berlin · Bruxelles · Chennai · Lausanne · Oxford

Bibliographic Information published by the Deutsche Nationalbibliothek
The Deutsche Nationalbibliothek lists this publication in the Deutsche Nationalbibliografie; detailed bibliographic data is available online at http://dnb.d-nb.de.

Library of Congress Cataloging-in-Publication Data
Library of Congress Control Number: 2025012684

Cover Image: Bashō-san the Lorekeeper
Cover design by Peter Lang Group AG.

ISSN «BSeries_ISSN»
ISBN 978-3-0343-5483-7 (Print)
ISBN 978-3-0343-5484-4 (ePDF)
ISBN 978-3-0343-5485-1 (ePUB)
DOI 10.3726/b22979

© 2026 Peter Lang Group AG, Lausanne (Switzerland)
Published by Peter Lang Publishing Inc., New York (USA)

info@peterlang.com

All rights reserved.
All parts of this publication are protected by copyright.
Any utilization outside the strict limits of the copyright law, without the permission of the publisher, is forbidden and liable to prosecution.
This applies in particular to reproductions, translations, microfilming, and storage and processing in electronic retrieval systems.

This publication has been peer reviewed.

www.peterlang.com

Table of Contents

List of Figures vii
Acknowledgments ix

Game Start: The NPC, the Frog, and the Infinite Void 1
Game Start: Ludus, StrataPlay, and the Lorekeeper 15
Player One: Contours of Cacophony 29
Player Two: Nourishing Legacies 45
Player Three: TnT the Word RPG 61
Player Four: The Ultimate X Collab™ 79
Player Five: Überfrau Manifesto 99
GG: Dumb Ways to Die as a Lorekeeper 121

Bibliography 125
Index 129

List of Figures

Figure 1.1. QR code for Lorekeeper's Playlist
(drmilaz.com/academic-otaku) 13

Acknowledgments

First and foremost, my deepest thanks go to Dr. Alison Jefferson and the entire team at Peter Lang for seeing the potential in this unconventional work. These chapters of our collective gameplay exist because of your unwavering belief and support.

A special nod of gratitude goes to Dr. M. Francyne Huckaby and Dr. Gabriel Huddleston at Texas Christian University, who have been guiding me through academia for an impressive 13 years. They also managed to hold me inside out at commencement, and I've been cursed ever since—still haven't figured out how the hood actually works. But hey, inside out and proud, right?

To Dr. Anatoly Oleksiyenko from the Education University of Hong Kong, the legendary cellist Mr. Jian Wang from the Shanghai Conservatory of Music, Dr. Sarah Watkins from the University of Auckland, Dr. Walter Gershon from Rowan University, and Prof. Jingbo Xu from Fudan University: your support has been an anchor, and for that, I will always be grateful.

I could easily entertain you with stories of how I'm surrounded by the most extraordinary colleagues, friends, mentors, and students at

Southeastern Oklahoma State University for at least three nights. To Dr. Stewart Mayers, Dr. David Whitlock, Dr. Teresa Golden, Dr. Jeremy Blackwood, Dr. Susan Ronnenberg, and Dr. Katheryn Shannon—thank you for being both my guides and cheerleaders. Special appreciation goes to the dynamic duo of the library, Andy Kramer and Jayanna Greenwood, as well as my comrades in the entire EIL department: Sally Jackson, David Wyatt, Dr. Sarah Morrison, Dr. Robert Shauger, Dr. Kathleen Boothe, Dr. Chaehyun Lee, Dr. Susan Morrison, Dr. Maribeth Nottingham, Dr. Jerry Stout, Dr. Todd Williams, Dr. Kalyn McAlester, Jennifer Arnold, Greg Masters, Kelli Norman, and our ever-helpful student assistant Danielle Paddor. And, of course, to my magical instructional assistant, Dr. Michelle Coates.

To my dear friends Zhihui Xie, Prof. Coven Maxwell, Natalie Weaver, Dr. Ying Wang, Amelia Wang, Dr. Jingjing Ma, Dr. Xiaoyan Wang, Dr. Chen Yuan, Wei Zhang, Shule Han, and Haiwen Liu—your absence is felt today, but your presence has always been essential. Special thanks to my brilliant friends and collaborators, soon-to-be Dr. David Penn, Steven Harris, Jason Stowell, and our unstoppable SEsports team—without you, the gamification of postqualitative inquiry might still be a distant dream.

And finally, with all my heart, to my parents and to the most inspiring, wonderful young man I know, my 9-year-old Claude—your light makes every day a joy.

Each of you has played a key role in this level-up, adding your own power-ups and secret moves to this quest, and for that, I thank you from the bottom of my heart.

Game Start

The NPC, the Frog, and the Infinite Void

I encountered one of the NPCs this morning—my unwitting harbinger of punctuality.

"Good morning, Professor," she chirped, her smile as broad as the dawn. The perfect antidote to the morning's solemnity, stationed just outside the ladies' room by the auditorium.

At that very moment, the campus clock tower sang the hour—eight strokes, clear and true.

This NPC, garbed in the humble attire of the cleaning crew, wields a power unmatched in this building. Keeper of keys, she unlocks all the essential gears and reveals the hidden levels of the realm (perhaps "sectors" or "zones" would better describe offices and classrooms in game settings?).

Spotting her is my little victory, a sign I've outpaced the clock—a rare feat, better than glimpsing the other NPC, the one who lives next door and appears much later, leisurely tending his garden with a sprightly Aussie shepherd at his side.

Oh, what, pray tell, is an NPC? For those of you unacquainted with the lexicon of gaming—particularly of the RPG (Role-Playing Game) variety—an NPC, or Non-Player Character, is a denizen of the game world. They are scripted souls, governed by the game's code rather than the caprice of human will, designed to guide, hinder, or merely populate the map through which players navigate.

This is your first clue that I am earnest about this scholarly project, which might not resemble one at first glance: elucidating gaming jargon for my dear readers who, quite possibly, picked up this book anticipating a treatise on postqualitative inquiry.

But brace yourselves, it gets more peculiar.

Sometimes, I feel as though the fourth wall has long been shattered. That we have already stepped into the cyborg prophecy many foresaw (Haraway, 1991; Turkle, 1995). As I walk down the aisle, I am graced with the tender and warm blessings of countless NPCs within this perceived reality. And perhaps, to you, I might appear as yet another NPC, too. In this intertwining of lives and narratives, we might all be playing parts in a much larger game.

For one who once dedicated six to eight hours daily to the demanding keys of a piano, it might seem curious that I now find myself nurturing pre-service teachers. My students anchor me firmly to the ground, preventing me from drifting entirely into anti-terrestrial realms. Despite this earthbound role, I still steal moments behind the stage right tormenter in the auditorium—mere steps from my office—where our institution harbors a rather splendid Bösendorfer. Not that such a confession is necessary, or even prudent, considering my supervisors might peruse these pages.

But there's something about that confined space. It holds an otherworldly charm under its dim, eerie lights—a perfect haven for brooding. There, amidst the shadows, one can truly muse over the ethereal aspects of, say, aesthetics. I recommend you try it; such brooding session on aesthetics usually extract you from the banalities of the everyday, offering a slice of solitude. And I dare say, your coiffure likely boasts more style than Schopenhauer's, and your regard for women surpasses his by leagues—given, of course, that you've picked up this book and are still with me, five hundred words in, without having flung it out the window.

One intriguing realization emerged during a recent self-remedial brooding session: the more I unwittingly encounter unchecked facts and rogue comments on social media, the more I find solace in conversing with frogs. Truly, frogs possess a poetic aura, sprinkled with a dry wit, and they are such attentive listeners. Unlike many of the human counterparts, they engage in dialogue merely to showcase their intellect or to highlight my supposed ignorance. No, these creatures are the epitome of thoughtful interlocutors, responding only after fully digesting one's words. Such refreshing exchange harkens back to the Socratic dialogues of Ancient Greece, where dialectical discussions weren't just academic exercises but pathways to understanding and democratic living (Cooper, 1999). Aristotle championed the concept of dialectic as a means of reaching philosophical truth, which suggests a society ripe with fair and productive debate. In such debates, participants engaged not for victory, but for progress, echoing the philosophical assemblies of old where ideas blossomed through the fertile soil of collective reasoning (Emerson, 2019). (Unlike the debates we now endure—reminiscent of two kindergarteners, each shouting on a seesaw, never meeting in the middle, or perhaps like mismatched socks endlessly tumbling in a dryer—the kind of discourse that could drive one to the brink of despair. But let me pause here, lest this book venture into the realm of the banned before its time. Not that such a fate would displease me. Indeed, joining the ranks of the proscribed would be a badge of honor, likening me to some legendary figures of forbidden lores.)

For now, I digress to more tranquil dialogues … with frogs. Truly, I kid you not. Just last week, amidst the chaos of countless inquiry emails—each plea for clarity **boldly** <u>underscored</u> and *italicized* in the <u>*syllabi*</u>—I sought refuge with my amphibious confidant. There, little

Bashō-san[1] ribbitted his wisdom in just 17 syllables (equivalent of eight and a half *ribbit*'s), a pause after the fifth and the twelfth syllables marking the rhythm. I could almost see the delicate structure of a haiku hovering above his head:

Bold lines underscored,
Queries whirl in autumn's breeze—
Read your syllabus.

My engaging in dialogue with frogs, through a posthumanist lens, may acquire some unexpected philosophical significance. Posthumanism challenges the anthropocentric hierarchies that traditionally separate human from non-human, mind from body, and culture from nature (Braidotti, 2013). By conversing with frogs, an act that on the surface subverts conventional academic seriousness, I embody the posthumanist critique of these binaries, suggesting a more fluid, interconnected existence. Such dialogues also resonate with posthuman feminist perspectives, which advocate for a reconfiguration of identity and agency that includes non-human actors. Haraway's (2016) notion of "making kin" with other forms of life invites us to consider these interspecies exchanges not as mere metaphorical constructs but as genuine interactions that destabilize the notion of the isolated, superior human subject. Through the delightfully timely Basho-san-esque haiku, one touches upon the core of posthuman feminism—acknowledging and

---

1   Matsuo Bashō (1644–1694) is one of the most celebrated poets of the Edo period in Japan. Renowned for his haiku, Bashō elevated this brief poetic form to a highly refined art through his exquisite sensitivity to nature and Zen-infused philosophy. Perhaps his most famous haiku, capturing both the serenity and the sudden activity in nature, goes like this:

   An old silent pond …
   A frog jumps into the pond—
   Splash! Silence again.

   In this book, when I refer to "little Basho-san," it is with a whimsical nod to Bashō's ability to capture profound thoughts in minimal words. The name "Basho-san" is affectionately applied to the frog companion of mine, linking the poet's name with the nature of the conversations I imagine having with my amphibian friend—inspired by Bashō's famous contemplation of a frog.

embracing the agency of the non-human in constructing a shared world. Moreover, engaging with the arts, particularly the discipline of poetry, provides a vehicle for transcending traditional epistemological boundaries (Abram, 1996). Poetry allows for the expression of complex ideas through minimalistic means and often serves as a bridge between the rational and the emotional, the scientific and the artistic. In such whimsical exchanges, I participate in a tradition that values brevity and precision while inviting contemplation of life's interconnectedness, echoing the posthumanist call for a deeper engagement with strata of narratives.

Back to the Shadows Behind the Curtain.

Hidden by the heavy drapes of the auditorium, I've stumbled upon another rather stark realization: I am hopelessly ignorant, and it's not a matter of self doubt. From my days as a bright-eyed protégée to my current role as a principal investigator, the more I've delved into the rigors of research—the endless cycles of literature reviews, observation, interviews, data analysis, and manuscript crafting—the more I've sensed an arrogant detachment creeping upon me. Now, about this detachment—the cacophony of bipartisan debates and relentless social media commentaries that further alienate me from my earlier zeal surely didn't help. But there's more. Foucault might argue it's symptomatic of our society's pervasive surveillance, where power insidiously observes and judges, turning us into mere subjects under its gaze (Foucault, 1977). I can feel my advocate persona—once vibrant and bold, championing the causes of the unheard and marginalized—fades. It's as if each piece of my conviction is chiseled away day by day, leaving me questioning the efficacy of my actions. Thus, the need for these brooding sessions, once a personal ritual, has dwindled. I find myself wondering if perhaps the wiser role is that of a detached observer, a spectator in the grand game of the universe, where the play unfolds with or without my interference.

In this bout of self-aware ignorance, there was a moment I considered ceasing to write, to halt leaving behind any trace of potential misfires. Consider Laozi, the ancient sage who was reticent to encapsulate his deep-seated reflections in words. Legend has it that it required the stubborn determination of a border guard and the promise of anonymity to coax from him the *Tao Te Ching*, a mere 5,000 words that would resonate through millennia (Kaltenmark, 1969). Not that I dare compare myself to Laozi, but my hesitation stemmed from a well-reasoned itch: the suspicion that true enlightenment lies not in the rigid preservation of thought, but in the fluidity of learning, unlearning, and relearning—a notion underscored by psychologist Herbert Gerjuoy and quoted by Alvin Toffler in his book, *Future Shock*, more than half a century ago, "The illiterate of the 21st century will not be those who cannot read and write, but those who cannot learn, unlearn, and relearn" (Toffler, 1970, p.414). This era demands knowledge as well as audacity to dismantle and reset the game. I crave the liberty to negate what I have once championed and to reclaim what I have renounced, without being fettered by my own past assertions. Hegel's dialectic, the thesis and antithesis leading to a synthesis, might offer a framework here, reflecting a dynamic where each idea inevitably gives rise to its opposite, only to reconcile in a higher form of understanding (Hegel, 1977). In this light, my fear of being bound by my own words reveals itself as a trap—an ongoing philosophical evolution that risks leaving behind a trail of utterances that could portray me, at best, as a capriciously changeable thinker, unstable and illogical.

One more realization unfurled during my brooding sessions in the confines of the auditorium. Here, enveloped in the theatrical, liminal embrace of this space, I found that extreme quietude is not so different from cacophonous chaos. It's a curious *interlude*, this solitude—not quite a rehearsal, not yet an open performance. My mind buzzed with thoughts as I found myself surrounded by both animate and inanimate spectators, none of us bound by a strict script. Perhaps, then, this is more akin to an improvisational act in an open theater, where all participants are equal thespians? This peculiar balance between the intense inner tumult, fueled by the relentless surge of information in this era of explosive technological advancement, and the serene detachment found in the quietude of my surroundings, seemed to crystallize a revelation. It was as if I were perpetually ensnared by the *Infinite Void*—infinitely close to the totality of knowledge and wisdom spanning all universes, yet still just out of reach, unable to grasp even a single shard of them.

This concept of the "Infinite Void," while uniquely depicted in popular culture such as in Gege Akutami's manga, *Jujutsu Kaisen*,[2] has philosophical roots that stretch across various traditions and epochs. In Eastern philosophy, particularly within Buddhism, there is the notion of *śūnyatā* or *emptiness*. This concept does not imply a mere absence but rather an expansive presence of infinite potentiality. Such emptiness is the foundational state from which all forms and phenomena arise and to which they return—an infinite reservoir of potential (Williams, 1989). Similarly, Taoist philosophy speaks of the "Dao" as an ineffable void, a source of boundless creation and the ultimate pathway to harmonious living (Laozi, 300 BCE). Western philosophy also delves into the concept of the void, though often with existential connotations. Nietzsche's discussions of the abyss suggest a void that "gazes back," a depth where traditional moral structures dissolve, leaving space for new values to emerge (Nietzsche, 1886). Heidegger (1927), too, explores the theme of nothingness, suggesting that an encounter with the void is intrinsic to understanding the very essence of being. Incorporating these philosophical underpinnings, the Infinite Void in my narrative can be seen beyond metaphysical space—it is a symbol of the constant flux of understanding and the elusive nature of knowledge in an era dominated by information overload. As I stand on the brink of this vast emptiness, the cacophony of the modern age echoes the paradoxical silence of the void: it is both nothingness and overflowing, a source of both tranquility and overwhelming noise.

Before I further entangle myself in these dichotomized musings on omniscience and ignorance, on emptiness and overflow, which might just stall the progress of this book—crafted, mind you, in our shared

---

2 Gege Akutami is the pseudonym of the Japanese manga artist known for creating *Jujutsu Kaisen*, a popular manga series that began serialization in 2018. One of the notable elements in Akutami's work is the concept of the "Infinite Void," a spell used by the character Satoru Gojo. This spell places its target in an expansive void where the normal laws of physics do not apply, overwhelming their senses with limitless nothingness, which is a unique interpretation of traditional Japanese folklore and Buddhist concepts interwoven with supernatural action. *Jujutsu Kaisen* has been praised for its complex characters, intricate plot, and its blending of dark fantasy with psychological depth.

game arena—I must digress to highlight an event that, in my humble opinion, might just be one of the best things happened in this perplexing post-pandemic era (or is it really "post" yet? Half of my class is out with COVID—what do we even call these times …? Borrowing inspiration from posthumanism, maybe we could dub these strange times the *Post-Presence Epoch*, where the very idea of human presence is continuously redefined, split between digital realms and physical spaces. In this Post-Presence Epoch, our existence is marked by simultaneous hyperconnectivity and estrangement, where even the concept of "being there" has transformed into something both tangible and virtual, biological and digital.)

Now, prepare for a twist: Sanrio, the iconic purveyor of cuteness, masterminded a strategic collaboration with none other than Junji Ito, the maestro of manga horror. This fall, they're launching pop-up stores in Tokyo and Osaka. Imagine that—a fusion of cuteness and creepy.

For your reference, *Sanrio*, founded in 1960, is renowned globally for its adorable characters, most famously *Hello Kitty*. This company has woven itself into the field of popular culture by creating characters that embody gentleness and charm, making the mundane delightful. Junji Ito, on the other hand, is a celebrated figure in the horror genre of manga. His works, such as "Uzumaki" and "Tomie,"[3] are acclaimed for their ability to evoke the sublime terror of the uncanny, marrying everyday settings with deeply unsettling narratives. This unexpected pairing between Sanrio's sweetness and Ito's spine-chilling tales is nothing short of an interdimensional spectacle, blurring the lines between genres in a way that only a true game-changer could.

It's as if Empiricism goes, "Bro, you're so vibey," and Rationalism claps back, "Nah fam, you're straight fire." Picture Apollonian deciding, "You know what? I'm tired. Let's throw caution to the wind and revel in spontaneous hedonism," while Dionysian, ever the contrarian, declares, "I'm bored of excess; let's adopt a stoic demeanor." Imagine

---

3   Junji Ito's manga series "Uzumaki" was originally serialized from 1998 to 1999, and "Tomie" was first published in 1987. These works are among his most famous, with "Uzumaki" exploring the surreal terror of a cursed spirals infesting a small town, and "Tomie" featuring an immortal girl who drives those around her to madness and murder.

Sisyphus, notorious for his cunning that tricked Death itself, finally tiring of his existential plight. Instead of eternally pushing his boulder (courtesy of Thanatos, the god of nonviolent deaths), he sets it aside to indulge in the simple pleasures of a good rom-com novel. Meanwhile, Thanatos, having become an aficionado of the absurd through his readings of Camus and Kafka, now spends his days contemplating the ironies of existence, utterly enchanted by the very absurdity that Sisyphus seeks to escape. Or envision Cyrano de Bergerac (Rostand, 1897), famed for his poetic soul and deft swordsmanship, turning his talents to Photoshop mastery. His Tinder profile pictures become a gallery of devilishly handsome portraits, each nose more impeccably edited than the last. Meanwhile, Christian, once reliant on Cyrano's silver tongue, heads off to graduate school, emerging as a professor with a trifecta of doctoral degrees in Art History, French Literature, and Library Science, dazzling his students with lectures that are as charming as they are erudite.

This captivating mashup of *kawaii*—often characterized by its cuteness, simplicity, and the ability to evoke happiness—and *kowai*—denoting a spine-chilling sense of horror that lurks beneath the surface—echoes Junji Ito's portrayal of Tomie. This paradoxical being embodies the coexistence of desire and detestation, and the juxtaposition of the infinite loop of destruction and rebirth creates a mesmerizing dance of contrasts that captivates and horrifies in equal measure.

Now, you might be curious, why am I prattling on about horror manga and Hello Kitty, channeling my inner nerdy nerd (… and unabashedly so)? The answer lies in the beauty of reconciling the seemingly irreconcilable—the extremes of the pendulum. When we embrace this synthesis, we begin to be kinder to ourselves. This reflection is an emancipatory revelation, deeply anchored in the scholarly discourse on nonviolence. Drawing upon the work of thinkers who explore the pedagogy of peace and the curricular significance of nonviolence (Wang, 2004, 2010, 2013; Pinar, 2023), we find that engaging with internal dualities—such as omniscience and ignorance, or emptiness and overflow—can significantly reduce internal conflict and foster self-acceptance. In particular, Pinar (2006, 2023) emphasizes that nonviolent relationality bridges inner and outer work, helping individuals transcend personal divisions and transform curriculum dynamics. Wang's (2013) concept of a "zero space of nonviolence" further supports this idea by illustrating how cultivating peace within ourselves can simultaneously create communal harmony, aligning with her broader framework of social justice education. She contends that nonviolence in education not only mitigates outward violence but also fosters deep personal integration, making the practice of self-compassion and genuine self-expression vital for both personal and societal transformation. Additionally, Mingfang He's work on reconciling cultural narratives (2003) enriches this dialogue by highlighting the transformational potential of embracing one's own cultural complexities. Engaging with these narratives within oneself, as He proposes, allows for a deeper understanding of personal and cultural identity. In this sense, writing down my fleeting but authentic thoughts is not only acceptable but essential for nonviolent self-acceptance and growth.

Moreover, integrating insights from Carl Rogers (1961), who championed the idea of unconditional positive regard within psychology, we see the therapeutic potential of self-forgiving writing as a means to nurture self-acceptance. Michel Foucault's exploration of self-care as an ethical practice further illuminates how writing authentically can also serve as a *technology of the self* (Foucault, 1988), a tool for shaping one's identity. Meanwhile, the expressivist school, particularly through the works of Peter Elbow (1973), argues for writing as a process of discovery and acceptance, where the act of writing itself is a forgiving encounter with one's thoughts and feelings. And concepts from Dialectical Behavior Therapy (Linehan, 1993) echo this sentiment, with its core principle of radical acceptance providing a framework for understanding the transformative power of writing that embraces all facets of the self. In this sense, writing emerges as a transformative space in this exploration of reconciling the irreconcilable. Embracing the oscillations of my own mind, whether I am engulfed in a moment of weariness desiring detachment, or swept by surges of empathy and compassion, the act of writing becomes a sanctuary for these transient truths. Nathan Snaza's engagement with the concept of "endarkenment," a state of embracing the unknown and unseen aspects of knowledge and existence, enriches this process. Writing captures the essence of the moment—fleeting and unfiltered. This recognition of the ephemeral nature of my thoughts and their expression in words aligns with Snaza's idea of dealing with "the hypothetical or the speculative," exploring *"ghostly regions* of thought" (Snaza, 2014, p.19). The ritual of writing, thus, is not merely cathartic but is fundamentally emancipatory that acknowledges the continuous unlearning and relearning of one's understanding of the universe. This dynamic where the known constantly makes way for the unknown, invites a broader, more inclusive understanding of the world, promoting a depth that celebrates the ambiguity and complexity of knowledge.

But even if I can conjure 101 reasons to persist in this self-inflicted saga—forever flirting with a sliver of truth in the pursuit of knowledge and the craft of writing, always tantalizingly *just out of reach* in the Infinite Void—I still sense a missing piece. It's something more profound than mere "courage" to balance the imbalanced or capture the endarkened, more intense than the perverse pleasure of enduring academia's lashing like a seasoned masochist. It's akin to a musical motif, a cross-dimensional collab like the Junji Ito X Hello Kitty, which sparks an electric jolt of inspiration. This puzzle piece, I believe, leads to the proposal of *StrataPlay* as my shift of thinking in qualitative inquiry. The question that haunts us isn't merely how researchers, storytellers, narrators, and participants endure but how we thrive amidst the cacophony of destructive, soul-crushing discourses that permeate our era. These discourses include the relentless grind of neoliberalism, which commodifies every aspect of life; the ever-present specter of global conflicts that drain our collective spirit; and the existential threat of environmental degradation, which casts a long shadow over our shared future. How do we keep the spirit of inquiry alive and vibrant in such a context?

Glancing at the clock, I rose, ready to conclude this session of brooding soliloquy. The student worker would soon be bustling through the door, heralding the start of my office hours. Ah, September! Beloved by many, not only for the frenzied onset of a new semester but also as the unofficial opener of the Halloween season. Have I mentioned I've been itching to unveil my costume for this year's library cosplay contest since last Halloween? Yes? More than once? Let's skip past that then. The point is, we all crave these outlets—a chance to unveil hidden facets of ourselves, whether a single layer or several, through the playful guise of "cosplay." It's as if we're all understudies momentarily stepping into the spotlight, revealing slices of truth in a gamified theater filled with fellow thespians.

If only I could perpetuate this game across all narratives, in those complex inter-dimensional spaces where traditional terminologies falter. Data collection? Human subjects? Those terms seem almost quaint in this epoch. I yearn for real conversations held within games that embrace inclusivity, warmth, and above all, authenticity, no matter how absurd or decidedly unconventional the form may appear. Yet, it's precisely these absurd and unconventional forms that prompt us to question what is deemed normal or acceptable, pushing us toward a broader understanding of reality. This stepping beyond conventional boundaries is a necessary leap into realms where creativity and innovation thrive. Here, in the interstitial spaces between the known and the unknown, lies the potential for meaningful transformation through that one missing piece, *escapism*.

Escapism, often misconstrued merely as a flight from reality, holds a far more constructive role in the human psyche. It provides a sanctuary where the rigid confines of the perceived reality melt away, allowing for a playful exploration of identity and possibility. In this realm, the boundaries between self and other, real and imagined, dissolve, offering a space where transformative learning and self-(re)discovery can occur. As D. W. Winnicott articulated (1971), play and the imaginative spaces it creates are vital for both children and adults, serving as a developmental stage where the self is realized and reimagined. Moreover, the concept of escapism aligns with Johan Huizinga's notion of the "magic circle" of play, a term Huizinga (1949) uses to describe the special, isolated experience of gameplay that is set apart from ordinary life. Within this circle, players engage in activities that follow different rules from those of their everyday existence, facilitating a type of learning and interaction that is both distinct from and reflective of their real lives. This theoretical framework underscores the importance of escapism in fostering an environment where traditional barriers are temporarily suspended, and participants are free to explore identities and scenarios.

Within such framework, every study has the potential to morph into a game, and every participant—from researchers to subjects—becomes a player. Yet, researchers, in their quintessential roles, don the mantle of more: keepers of lores, designers of game systems, singing narratives with heartfelt gusto. This game-based worldview strips away the rigidity often associated with research, restoring a sense of ease and fluidity that invites more natural interactions and discoveries. Imagine a reality where the line between the narrative and the everyday blurs—where NPCs, frogs, and Hello Kitty are as warm and genuine as the trivia behind Junji Ito's collaboration with Sanrio. (Apparently, Ito initially thought the idea was outlandish, driven only by the whims of attention economy. However, influenced by his wife and daughter—ardent Sanrio enthusiasts—he embraced the partnership, hoping it might somehow boost his domestic status, much to my amusement.) The warmth and genuineness behind each and every element are a vivid reminder of the absurdity in upholding the *centrality* of human beings. In a gamified reality, these characters are not mere figments or fictional creations; they are tangible, integral to the narratives, each playing their part in debunking the myth of human exceptionalism.

All this to say, dear players, let's not rush the dice. The game is merely at its dawn, and I'm here to unveil the lore-rich backstory of becoming a Lorekeeper and unravel the game settings of the StrataPlay methodology. For those audiophiles among you, craving a melody to accompany your journey through these pages, feel free to scan this QR code for some tailor-made tunes—a little playful gift from yours truly.

Figure 1.1. QR code for Lorekeeper's Playlist (drmilaz.com/academic-otaku).

Also, as your bard-in-training and self-proclaimed Lorekeeper, I've woven narratives to craft a ballad befitting the opening of an RPG that might just make our scholarly quest feel like an epic adventure.

Ballad of the Lorekeeper: The Opening Quest

Beneath the tower's chime at dawn's first light,
Keepers of keys, cloaked in morning's quiet grace,
Greets with a smile, their spirit bright,
The NPCs, guardians of this sacred place.

In shadows where echoes softly tread,
A frog leaps forth from silent, verdant beds.
With whispers of wisdom subtly spread,
In haikus hung, where curious minds are led.

Oh, venture deep into the Infinite Void,
Where knowledge weaves like threads of fate employed,
An endless map, finely alloyed,
With tales of old, in new dimensions now enjoyed.

Through corridors of time, past doors unseen,
Walks the Lorekeeper, through realms between.
With every step, a story gleaned—
Of life and lore in the gamified scene.

Where scholars play with boundless zest,
Unearthing truths on this grand quest,
In StrataPlay, we dance in jest,
To balance scales, we choose our test.

So take this to me, dear wandering soul,
Embrace the game, let wonder unroll,
For in each page, you'll find the whole—
A universe within a scholar's scroll.

Game Start

Ludus, StrataPlay, and the Lorekeeper

#Dumb Ways to Die as a Lorekeeper

Falling into the posthuman abyss,
Thinking this was a quant study—what a miss,
Over-interpreting everything,
While the narrative's supposed to sing.

Forgot I'm the Lorekeeper in this maze,
Daydreaming about dismembering players,
Turned into a dung beetle, what a fall,
Posthumanism consumed me, after all.

Chorus:
Dumb ways to die, so many dumb ways to die,
Dumb ways to die as a Lorekeeper in Thoughtspire.

The rest of this absurd Lorekeeper anthem, *Dumb Ways to Die as a Lorekeeper*, can be found in the final chapter, "Good Game." But if you're tempted to skip ahead to see just how the Lorekeeper meets her tragicomic demise, I suggest you resist—after all, none of it will make any sense without first losing yourself in the games of StrataPlay. So, for now, pause, take a breath, and let's dive into the theoretical bedrock of this labyrinthine methodology.

Postqualitative Inquiry: A Framework for StrataPlay

Postqualitative inquiry (PQI) represents a decisive turn away from traditional qualitative research, breaking free from predefined structures and methodologies. It invites fluid, dynamic approaches that acknowledge the complexity and multiplicity of lived experiences, embracing emergence rather than seeking closure (St. Pierre, 2011). This methodological openness resonates with theorists like Patti Lather and Elizabeth St. Pierre, who advocate for inquiry that disrupts the quest for fixed truths. Instead, PQI recognizes knowledge as a constant becoming, formed through entanglements of power, discourse, and materiality (Lather, 2013; St. Pierre, 2016). In this framework, knowledge is no longer a commodity to be mined or discovered but is instead co-constructed, relational, and always in flux. As Rosiek (2024) suggests in his exploration of postqualitative methods, the boundaries between researcher and researched dissolve, creating an ontological shift where the researcher becomes a participant, and the participant, in turn, becomes a co-creator of knowledge. The resulting inquiry is speculative, emergent, and often unpredictable, destabilizing any pretense of a singular, objective truth. Postqualitative inquiry thus demands not merely a methodological shift but an ontological one, where the very nature of knowing is reconsidered. We are no longer uncovering hidden meanings or universal truths; instead, we are immersed in the act of becoming, where knowledge is relational, always contingent, and deeply embedded in the entanglements of material-discursive flows (Barad, 2007).

The StrataPlay Ethos: Embodying Multiplicity and Emergence

StrataPlay, proposed in this book as a postqualitative methodology, embraces this ontological shift by turning the research process itself into a dynamic, narrative-driven, game-like experience. At its core,

StrataPlay refuses the hierarchical binaries that traditional research often perpetuates—such as subject/object, researcher/researched, and even player/narrative. In StrataPlay, the *Lorekeeper* (researcher) and the *player* (participant) do not "find" meaning; they create it through their interactions, choices, and interpretations. This is where the game aspect becomes crucial: just as a game requires continuous engagement, decision-making, and re-interpretation, so too does StrataPlay require researchers and participants to remain in a state of fluid interaction with knowledge and meaning. Knowledge does not flow in linear trajectories but proliferates through interconnected nodes (Deleuze & Guattari, 1987), producing new possibilities at every turn. Each interaction within the game creates new strata of meaning—layers that build, collapse, and reassemble in ways that defy closure. Players are encouraged to navigate these strata, not as passive recipients of knowledge, but as active co-creators, engaging in a "nomadic" form (Braidotti, 2013) of subjectivity—always in motion, always becoming.

StrataPlay embraces the idea of a "playground of becoming." Here, knowledge is not solidified or fixed but is always in process, always *becoming-with* the players, narratives, and the environments in which they are situated. This aligns with Barad's (2007) notion of intra-action, where entities (whether human, material, or discursive) co-constitute one another in ongoing processes of becoming. Through StrataPlay, research becomes a speculative act, a *what-if* of narrative exploration where meaning emerges as a momentary constellation of possibilities. Barad's (2007) theory of *agential realism* reframes traditional notions of causality and separateness, proposing that entities do not preexist their interactions. Instead, she offers the concept of *intra-action*, in which subjects and objects, human and non-human, do not exist as independent entities but come into being through their entangled relationships. In this framework, meaning, identity, and knowledge emerge *through* interaction. Similarly, the Lorekeeper, the players, the narrative, and the theoretical context in StrataPlay are not separate; rather, they are mutually co-constituted through intra-action. This means that the narrative is not just something that players narrate and lorekeepers interpret, but something that comes into being *with* them. The player does not merely *read* the narrative, nor does the narrative exist *before* lorekeepers engage with it; instead, the two emerge together through play, intra-acting in ways that create new possibilities for meaning and understanding.

Meanwhile, the narrative's material-discursive components—the text, the theoretical concepts, the choices players make—are not simply static "pieces" of the game. They intra-act with the players' choices and reflections, creating something entirely new each time a game is played. This ongoing process of intra-action mirrors the posthumanist idea that identities and meanings are not fixed or essential but are instead constantly shifting and becoming.

Reimagining Posthumanism through StrataPlay

Posthumanism, particularly in the work of scholars like Donna Haraway, invites us to rethink the boundaries between the human, the non-human, and the more-than-human world. Haraway's concept of the Chthulucene (2016) offers a way to move beyond the Anthropocene's narrow focus on human impact and instead foreground multispecies entanglements, symbiotic relationships, and ecological kinship. In this framework, human beings are not the central actors of the world but are instead deeply entangled with non-human forces, constantly interacting and evolving within shared ecosystems.

StrataPlay draws its inspiration from these posthumanist insights, creating a methodological space where identity, knowledge, and agency are not centered on the human subject but are distributed across a network of interactions—between human, non-human, and even narrative elements. This unique methodology breaks free from the anthropocentric focus of traditional research and game design, exploring how identity and agency are fluid, relational, and often shaped by forces beyond the human. In *Player Three: TnT the Word RPG* and *Player Five: Überfrau Manifesto*, StrataPlay invites players to step into a labyrinth where the boundaries between self and other blur, and where posthumanist themes—such as multiplicity, fluidity, and the rejection of binary thinking—become central to gameplay. In "Thoughtspire," the setting for these chapters, players interact with absurd and philosophical challenges, confronting their own fragmented identities while engaging with non-human and hybrid forces. For example, in

Player Five: Überfrau Manifesto, players grapple with the concept of the Überfrau, a fluid, evolving identity that defies the static ideals of human perfection. The Überfrau embodies both the vulnerabilities and the strengths of posthumanism—she exists in a state of constant becoming, shaped by her interactions with the world around her. In this context, StrataPlay reflects Haraway's emphasis on multispecies kinship by encouraging players to move beyond fixed notions of individuality, embracing instead the interconnectedness of all beings, whether human or non-human. In addition, the designed gameplays' narrative-driven structure, where players co-create meaning through their choices, mirrors the posthuman idea that no being exists in isolation. Every interaction within the game is an entangled process of becoming, where human and non-human forces, cultural discourses, and theoretical insights combine to produce new identities and forms of knowledge. Through these entanglements, StrataPlay dissolves the human/non-human divide, illustrating that knowledge is not a product of individual insight but a relational process that unfolds through interaction.

By drawing on posthumanism, StrataPlay offers players a dynamic, fluid approach to identity and knowledge creation, one that reflects the complexities of a world where the human is no longer the sole agent. Instead, the game setting positions lorekeepers and players as part of a broader network of entanglements, where identities are co-constructed and knowledge emerges not from a single source but from the interactions between all elements within the system.

Posthumanism & Fragmented Identity

The concept of fragmented identity is a central theme in *Player Five: Überfrau Manifesto*. As players navigate the game's challenges, they are invited to confront the idea that identity is not singular or static, but fluid, fragmented, and constantly evolving. The Überfrau—a key figure in this chapter—represents the complexity of modern identity, which is shaped by competing desires, vulnerabilities, and external expectations. The Überfrau resists any singular definition, embodying both strength and vulnerability, autonomy and conformity, visibility and invisibility. Through the gameplay, players are invited to explore these tensions within themselves, grappling with their own fragmented sense of self. This theme of fragmentation draws on posthumanist theories, which emphasizes this interconnectedness, arguing that human identity is entangled with the non-human and more-than-human world, forming webs of existence that resist simple categorization. StrataPlay's such focus on fragmented identities also draws upon Julia Kristeva's (1982) theory of *abjection*, which explores the disruption of the borders between the self and the other. *Abjection* reflects the discomfort that arises when these boundaries are blurred—when the self confronts aspects of itself that it finds both repulsive and alluring. In StrataPlay, players face these boundaries head-on, encountering "shards" of their fragmented selves and grappling with the parts of their identity that are simultaneously *desired* and *despised*, *visible* and *vulnerable*. This confrontation with the abject forces players to reckon with their own fluidity, acknowledging the uneasy, often chaotic process of becoming.

Jacques Lacan's (1982) *mirror stage* theory further enriches this understanding of fragmented identity. Lacan describes the moment in early childhood when one first recognizes themselves in a mirror—an idealized image that represents a unified self. However, this reflection is a mirage, one that the individual will perpetually strive toward but never fully achieve. In StrataPlay, this tension plays out as players navigate the game setting, confronted with distorted, fractured reflections of themselves that never quite align with their own sense of identity. Meanwhile, Michel Foucault's (1975) theory of *panopticism* adds yet another layer to the complexity of identity under surveillance. Foucault examines how individuals internalize the constant gaze of authority, shaping their behavior as if they are perpetually being watched. In StrataPlay, this manifests through challenges where players must perform under the weight of multiple, often conflicting gazes. The tension between the desire to be seen and the need to remain hidden fractures the player's identity, as they are pulled in different directions by external expectations and internal desires.

In short, StrataPlay creates a dynamic, shifting gaming arena where identities are fragmented, fluid, and always in the process of becoming. It rejects the notion of a fixed or essential self, instead inviting players to embrace the complexity and ambiguity of their identities—identities that are shaped by entanglements with the non-human world. In the postqualitative and posthumanist framework, StrataPlay offers a space where the self is never singular or complete, but always evolving, relational, and contingent upon the myriad forces that shape it.

Overview of the Five Gameplays

With the groundwork of StrataPlay laid out, it's time to delve into the game setting itself. Each chapter of this book represents a different level of engagement with the core ideas of postqualitative inquiry, posthumanism, and fragmented identity, with the players navigating complex gaming arenas of meaning, theory, and self-discovery. Through gameplay and theoretical reflection, each chapter invites you, dear reader, to embrace a different facet of the evolving *Überfrau*. These chapters are academic exercises as well as embodied experiences. In the following overview, we will explore how each of the five gameplays in StrataPlay unfolds, highlighting the unique challenges and insights they offer. As you step into this journey, remember: the paths ahead are winding, absurd, and unpredictable. Let the games begin.

Player One: Contours of Cacophony

Synesthesia, Loss of Hearing, and Narrative Identity

Imagine a world where sound and sight blur together—a reality where each note of music is not only heard but seen, felt, and absorbed by every part of you. For me, it began with the simple act of sitting at the piano, blissfully unaware that my ears carried a unique gift: perfect pitch. What started as a curious quirk became the defining trait of my identity, celebrated by those around me as though I held the keys to a rare and precious secret. But what happens when that gift—so integral to your sense of self—begins to fade?

Player One explores the contours of identity through the lens of sensory loss, specifically the unraveling of my own auditory world. In this chapter, we dive into the psychological and emotional impact of losing a defining ability and how it reshapes one's sense of self. The game design for *Contours of Cacophony* brings this experience to life through synesthetic gameplay—immersing the player in a theater of sound, touch, and silence. Our Player One, Bea, a former virtuoso pianist, struggles with physical limitations, much like my own loss of hearing, and navigates a world where music is no longer the domain of sound alone. In *Contours of Cacophony*, the player engages in tactile interactions with instruments, synesthetic puzzles that blend light, sound, and vibration, and adaptive dialogue with the Lorekeeper. The game mirrors the player's real-life limitations, offering a space to reflect on loss, adaptation, and the shifting boundaries of identity. As you play, you'll be asked to confront the fundamental question: *Who are we when we lose the very thing that defines us?*

Through theoretical frameworks like Merleau-Ponty's phenomenology and de Beauvoir's existentialism, this chapter explores how sensory disruptions force us to renegotiate our relationship with the world. The game challenges players to reimagine their identities not through the lens of deficit, but through transformation—finding meaning in the spaces between loss and possibility. As you step into *Player One*, you'll experience the synesthetic dance of sound and silence, the tactile resonance of identity in flux, and the infinite journey of becoming.

Player Two: Nourishing Legacies

Trauma, Motherhood, and Stuffed Grape Leaves

What can food tell us about the stories we carry, the trauma we inherit, and the identities we forge in the kitchen? In *Player Two: Nourishing Legacies*, the act of cooking becomes a journey through cross-generational trauma, identity reconstruction, and the nurturing role of motherhood.

At the heart of this game is Player Two, Nana, a mother who has lived through both personal and inherited trauma. Now raising her daughter while juggling her role as a full-time teacher, she grapples with the weight of past generations and the expectations of her present. The kitchen, often a space of comfort, becomes a battleground for reconciling her identity as a mother and an individual—each dish she prepares, a metaphor for the struggles she faces. In this culinary game, players select ingredients from a set of metaphorical index cards. Each ingredient represents an emotional layer, a memory, or a challenge. Stuffed grape leaves symbolize tightly held traditions, bitter melon speaks to the sharpness of inherited pain, and braised lamb represents the slow, tender growth of love. As our player construct a 12-course meal, they are also crafting a story of resilience, care, and transformation.

The game, set in a kitchen, allows the player to explore how food can nourish the body and the soul. The Lorekeeper, acting as a gentle guide, helps the player draw connections between the ingredients and their emotional journey, emphasizing how food represents both care and the complex legacies of trauma. Through the gameplay, players witness the player's evolution—her struggle to balance tradition with autonomy, and her desire to create a new future for her daughter, free from the burdens of the past.

Incorporating theoretical frameworks from postqualitative inquiry, *Nourishing Legacies* explores how embodied metaphors of food can serve as tools for storytelling and self-discovery. As Marianne Hirsch's (1997) concept of postmemory suggests, trauma is often passed down through generations, shaping identities even when the original experiences are not directly lived. In Player Two's case, food becomes a means of confronting that inherited trauma, using each dish as a step toward reclaiming her sense of self. Ultimately, *Nourishing Legacies* is a deeply personal exploration of motherhood, resilience, and the stories that shape us. Through the metaphors of food and the act of cooking, the player engages in a process of emotional healing and identity reconstruction. And if you're lucky, there might even be a Happy Meal involved. But just to warn you, the Kuromi toy is never guaranteed.

Player Three: TnT the Word RPG

Neal Libertas and the Post-Edu Apocalypse

Welcome to Thoughtspire, an interdimensional maze where academia, language, and reality have lost all meaning. In *Player Three: TnT the Word RPG*, you are no longer bound by the rules of logic or even time. This is a place where words twist into paradoxes, and nothing behaves as it should—think Beckett meets Kafka, with a dash of post-educational disaster. At the heart of this chapter is *Neal Libertas*, a monstrous embodiment of you-know-who, devouring campuses in his wake, reshaping education into a marketplace where students are customers, and schools are merely businesses.

In this absurd role-playing game, you, the player, are tasked with surviving the collapse of the educational system. Enrollment? Zero. Assignments? Zero. Yet, your mission remains to deliver a "world-class education." The absurdity mounts as you face a series of impossible challenges—such as attending conferences on a $0 budget or navigating a faculty meeting where the discussion revolves around providing education for nonexistent students. Alongside your fellow players, Beckett, Juliet, and Player IX, you'll be pushed to the brink of sanity as you unravel the nonsensical workings of a post-apocalyptic university.

At its core, this chapter explores how the neoliberal pressures of productivity and efficiency distort education, reducing it to a business venture devoid of purpose. Through its Magical-Post-Realism framework, *Player Three: TnT the Word RPG* blends magical realism, postmodernism, and posthumanism to reflect the surreal disconnection between academia's ideals and its realities under neoliberalism. The game becomes a philosophical journey, where the labyrinth of Thoughtspire mirrors the paradoxes of modern education—a system perpetually collapsing under its own contradictions.

Throughout the chapter, you'll learn about Neal Libertas, whose autobiography is retold in multiple genres—from Shakespearean tragedy to meme-filled Gen Alpha speak. Each retelling critiques a different facet of its grip on education, offering absurd yet biting commentary on how institutions have strayed from their purpose. And if that isn't enough, you'll also face the ultimate transformation: becoming a dung beetle tasked with rolling your ball of academic discourse, only to discover that, perhaps, there is no escape from life's absurdity.

So, will you accept the challenge, dear player? Step into Thoughtspire, where your only certainty is that nothing makes sense, and every turn is a new paradox.

Player Four: The Ultimate X Collab™

Bromance, the Fan Page, and the Zen Vibe

Welcome to the wildest mashup of cultural chaos imaginable—*Player Four: The Ultimate X Collab™* is where sense and reason are left behind in favor of inappropriate analogies, improbable collaborations, and poetic disasters. This chapter is an irreverent critique of how teaching analogies often fail, and instead of fostering understanding, they reinforce stereotypes and cultural centrality. But in *Player Four*, we're making a game out of critiquing this phenomenon.

Imagine this: You're tasked with creating the most improbable, farfetched cultural mashups possible. Ever imagined Athena and Guanyin joining forces with Joan of Arc to form a K-Pop girl group, all while Elizabeth Bennet choreographs their debut track? No? Well, you will now. Each challenge is designed to push the boundaries of plausibility, all while highlighting the ridiculousness of trying to make cultural analogies "fit" into a neat little box.

In *Folklore Mashup™*, you'll draw cards from East and West, creating bizarre collaborations between characters from wildly different mythologies and cultural stories. The results? Utterly nonsensical, but immensely fun. Then comes *K-Pop Reigns™*, where you're tasked with forming a K-Pop band out of characters from global folklore. Will Elizabeth Bennet take the lead dancer position? Will Athena, goddess of wisdom, become the group's main rapper? Anything is possible in this dazzling, chaotic world of cross-cultural musical absurdity.

Finally, the game culminates in *Poetic Translation Fail™*, a challenge where you attempt to translate vastly different forms of poetry. What happens when you try to squeeze Wordsworth's grandiose Romanticism into the rigid form of a Haiku? Or when a simple Zen poem is reimagined with Texan cowboy flair? Somewhere in the chaos, you might stumble across literary brilliance—or you might just resign yourself to the absurdity of it all.

Beyond the fun, *Player Four: The Ultimate X Collab™* digs deeper into the consequences of educational shortcuts—how simplistic analogies can distort rather than illuminate. Drawing from postcolonial theory and posthumanism, this chapter critiques how such analogies, especially those rooted in Western-centric thinking, reduce the complexity of cultural narratives into easily digestible stereotypes. As players, you'll confront this head-on, while simultaneously being invited to laugh at how utterly impossible it is to make sense of it all.

So, if you're ready to throw logic out of the window and let cultural icons dance across the stage of absurdity, then welcome to *The Ultimate X Collab*™. You might not walk away with clarity, but you'll definitely leave with a story worth telling.

Player Five: Überfrau Manifesto

The Wolf, the Shards, and Storytelling Stories

Step into *Player Five*, where visibility and vulnerability collide, and the weight of expectations fractures identity into countless pieces. Welcome to the *Überfrau Manifesto*, a hauntingly surreal game where *you—the player V—*are both protagonist and prey, caught in the gaze of the Lorekeeper. As the spotlight burns brighter, the boundaries of who you are begin to blur, fragmenting into shards of desire, fear, autonomy, and control.

The challenge? You must navigate this chaotic world of hypervisibility, performing for the relentless gaze of the Lorekeeper and the other fractured characters that haunt this space. They are here to watch you bend, break, and transform under pressure, pushing you to your limits as you try to reconcile the pieces of yourself scattered throughout Thoughtspire.

In *The Masquerade of Validation*, you will dance for masked figures—each one demanding a different version of you. Will you twist yourself to meet their expectations? Or will you resist the pull to conform? With every step, the Lorekeeper's gaze follows you, her admiration tinged with a darker edge. She wants to corrupt you, mold you into something more malleable (but she leaves you just enough slack to believe you're still in control.)

Then comes *Shards of You*, where the mirrors lining the labyrinth reflect not your physical self, but every fragmented version of your identity. The *Desired* you. The *Despised* you. The *Visible* you. The *Vulnerable* you. *Kuromi, Tomie,* and the Lorekeeper all take the stage in a twisted theater of fractured selves, each embodying a different aspect of your identity. It's up to you to decide: will you attempt to piece yourself back together? Or will you embrace the chaos of being torn apart?

As you move deeper into the game, the question that lies at the heart of *Überfrau Manifesto* becomes clear: Can you exist as a fluid, evolving entity, constantly shaped by the gaze of others without being destroyed by it? The *Überfrau* isn't a static ideal to be achieved, but a shifting, dynamic state of being—one that defies easy categorization. She is both predator and prey, both powerful and fragile, constantly navigating the contradictions inherent in being visible and vulnerable.

This chapter pulls no punches. It asks you to confront the darkest parts of yourself and the world around you, blurring the lines between player and Lorekeeper, self and other, autonomy and control. So, are you ready to step into the spotlight, dear player? The stage is set, the game is waiting. But beware: in Thoughtspire, every choice you make reveals a new shard of yourself—*and not all of them are easy to look at.*

Player One

Contours of Cacophony
Synesthesia, Loss of Hearing, and Narrative Identity

Nobody. Absolutely nobody.
Me: "I have perfect pitch."

It didn't seem like much when I first sat at the piano at three and a half, blissfully unaware that my ears had something special. But the moment my first piano teacher and my dad caught wind of it, they treated it like a divine gift—a blessing from above. For them, this was no mere quirk; it was a sign, a marvel to be showcased. They made sure to flaunt it, inviting me to perform for colleagues, peers, and at recitals. The performances were always elaborate, for dramatic effect, of course. I'd turn around or, better yet, wear a mask to prove I wasn't cheating—just for that extra flair. They'd graciously offer me an A440 as a reference (not that I needed it, really), and then the fun began. Intervals, triads, seventh chords—you play it, I'd name it. To me, it was as simple as breathing.

And then came the applause. People would cheer and marvel, like I'd just pulled a rabbit out of a hat. Some questioned if I was cheating, insisting on checking my mask to make sure I wasn't peeking. To be honest, I had no idea what all the fuss was about. It was just the way I was wired, nothing more, nothing less.

There's something peculiar about the English verb "play." Have you ever paused to consider how misleading it can be? Everything is *play*—play the piano, play the violin. It's as if the language itself is conspiring to make music seem like a carefree, lighthearted game. In Chinese, you *strike* the piano (弹琴 tán qín), and in Japanese, you *pull* the violin (ピアノを弾く piano wo hiku). If we said "strike the piano" or "pull the violin" in English, it would surely raise some eyebrows. The connotation behind "play," to some, implies a sense of ease and enjoyment, as if learning an instrument were as simple as hopscotch. But here's the catch: *play* isn't always about fun. In fact, the idea that play equals enjoyment is a rather modern, and somewhat deceiving, connotation. Memorization and repetition—those inevitable pillars of mastery—don't come wrapped in glitter and rainbows. As much as Gen Alpha might quip "This is lowkey not it" or roll their eyes at "a vibe … of boredom," the hours of grinding away at scales and exercises sit squarely, despite at the base of Bloom's taxonomy. Long before improvisation or interpretation, there's the unglamorous repetition, the process of embedding patterns in the mind (Erickson, 2018). Educational theory, especially from constructivists like Piaget (1962) and Vygotsky (1978), often emphasizes the importance of engaged (not joyous) play in learning. Play is not synonymous with enjoyment. No magic wand can bypass the hard work. Structured practice is essential because the brain needs patterns to grasp onto, and that requires effort, even when it's repetitive (Ericsson et al., 1993; Brown et al., 2014). The goal isn't always to have fun; rather, it's to immerse, to de-objectify the learning participants, to make the grind more meaningful, more personal.

This is one myth that prompts the StrataPlay methodology. *Play* is about creating a space where the challenges and the suffering of lives and lived experiences become more voiceable, more authentic. It's about engaging deeply in the process, not to sugarcoat the struggle, but to make it less daunting by turning it into a shared, immersive experience. In the end, "StrataPlay" is to dive into the depths of discovery, to make the research study a personal and shared journey.

Leaving aside the choice of verbs in the English language for now, I suppose I'm living proof that self-perception can be socially constructed and taught. Our identities are shaped by the narratives we internalize, whether we realize it or not (Gergen, 1991; Mead, 1934). Despite my initial indifference, the fuss and the accolades surrounding my perfect pitch slowly nudged me toward believing this was something to be … proud of? People have dreamt of possessing this talent, and yet I was simply born with it. Over time, it became part of me—so inextricably woven into my identity that it felt as natural as the comma Ph.D. that now follow my name. There was a time when I believed that if you knew me or respected me, it was because of this perfect pitch thingy—a built-in feature of the overall package. I never questioned whether it was okay to take it for granted. Why would I? I've always had sharp ears—so sharp that I can hear a phone buzzing from across a lecture hall. My hearing became a secret superpower, compensating for my less-than-stellar eyesight and questionable facial recognition skills. Hours spent squinting at those tadpole-shaped notes wriggling across glaring white pages in poorly lit rooms have punished my right eye down to a –7.50, while my left eye clearly decided it couldn't be outdone and went even blinder out of spite.

I've never told you this, but sometimes I really … can't see you. But I can hear you. I hear you to see you. It's a bit like when you're in a chaotic parking lot, and finding an open space feels as elusive as spotting a unicorn, so naturally, you lower the music … because surely that helps you see better. And I'm saying that with a straight face.

And just like that, I cleverly explained how the mechanism of synesthesia works to you.

Synesthesia, often described as a "cross-wiring" of the senses, occurs when stimulation of one sensory pathway leads to automatic, involuntary experiences in a second sensory pathway (Cytowic, 2002). This blending of sensory experiences—such as hearing colors or tasting sounds—offers insights into how our brains process and interpret sensory information. Synesthetic experiences can enhance creativity and perception, making them a frequent topic in artistic and musical circles (Ward, 2013). In my case, while I'm not a classic synesthete, I've often felt that sound and vision are inextricably linked, especially when

I'm *hearing* to *see*. My early fascination with these sensory overlaps led me to dive deeper into synesthetic experiences during my college years. These experiments explored the intersection of sound, art, and perception, driven by the philosophy that "the great sound is scarcely voiced, and the great image has no form" (Laozi, 300 BCE). They were my way of making sense of a world where sound and vision, form and formlessness, constantly intertwined. This fascination with the invisible lines between senses led me to one of the most ambitious projects 20 years back when my curiosity about synesthetic experiences was ascending. From such curiosity, *Contours of Silence* was born—a project that would push my exploration of Laozi's philosophy into new artistic territories.

The original *Contours of Silence*, subtitled "Eight Thousand Miles of Love," was a project that captured the very essence of Laozi's philosophy—seeking the formless form of sound through visual arts and theater performance. It's rather (ironically) poetic, how back then, when my ears were still sharp, I longed for silence. I found solace in Laozi's teachings, immersing myself in the pursuit of interpreting sound visually, bringing the intangible to life. With a stellar team—one talented music engineer, the chair of the student theater club, and a friend who was basically a human-shaped Doraemon[4] with an endless toolkit of skills—the project took shape smoothly.

Until, of course, the inevitable creative tensions surfaced. The framework was solid: the project was meant to represent life's journey, the search for meaning, and the arcs of identity. But when we reached the final movement, the question of how to wrap it up gnawed at us. The human Doraemon, ever the artist, vehemently opposed over-interpretation. He would nod sagely in agreement with Susan Sontag, who cautioned against digging too deeply for meaning. As Sontag

---

4 *Doraemon* is a beloved Japanese manga and anime character created by Fujiko F. Fujio. Doraemon is a robotic cat from the future, sent back in time to help a young boy navigate life. Equipped with an endless supply of futuristic gadgets from a fourth-dimensional pocket, Doraemon solves everyday problems with extraordinary inventions. Over the decades, *Doraemon* has become a cultural icon, representing innovation, problem-solving, and the charm of science fiction.

(1964) argued in *Against Interpretation*, art should be experienced as it is, in its raw, visceral form, without needing to dissect every layer to death. Doraemon wanted to celebrate the raw artistry of the performance, letting the audience make of it what they would. On the other hand, the theater chair was a stickler for structure. She insisted on a tightly knit format, complete with a coda that tied up every narrative thread we had woven from the start. To her, the arc needed a concrete ending—a wrap-up that felt satisfying and *conclusive*.

Then came the serendipitous breaking point, which was also the breakthrough: *Cyrano de Bergerac: Heroic Comedy in Five Acts* (Rostand, 1897). During one of our brainstorming sessions, we stumbled upon Cyrano's line, *Love is a journey with no destination, it is an infinite adventure*. Suddenly, it crystallized: what Doraemon and the theater chair were both striving for was the same harmonic resonance, expressed in different tonalities—the language of love. Rather than signaling a definitive closure, the coda became a philosophical gesture, echoing Nietzsche's notion of *eternal recurrence* (Nietzsche, 1998) and Bergson's concept of *duration* (*la durée*)—time not as linear progression but as a continuous unfolding of moments, each interwoven with love, creativity, and meaning. The essence of *Contours of Silence* was never meant to resolve, for life, as Bergson would remind us, is not about static points of closure but about perpetual becoming, a "creative evolution" (Bergson, 1907). The project's challenge thus lay not in crafting a finite narrative resolution, but in embracing the synesthetic unfolding of experiences that transcend both form and content, as Laozi's philosophy of *wúxíng* (无形)—the formless form—teaches us. Here, silence became the ultimate expression of life's endless adventure, an echo of Barthes' (1977) call to resist closure in favor of an open-ended text. The artistic process, like life, thrives in the space between the known and the unknown, the defined and the amorphous. Just as synesthesia intertwines sensory experiences, *Contours of Silence* became a fluid symphony of art, love, and life that transcended the finality of any singular note, embodying Derrida's (1967) concept of *différance*—the perpetual deferral of meaning—where love is not a destination but a continuous, infinite journey.

And the infinite journey went on.

You probably caught my drift earlier when I kept saying "back when my ears were still sharp." Well, sadly, those days are behind me, courtesy of a certain Omicron vibe that, quite literally, stole my perfect pitch. It started innocuously enough with tinnitus, then muffled sounds, until eventually, I was left with only half of my hearing capacity. I told the ENT doctor I was a musician, that I kinda, sorta needed my ears. She nodded sympathetically and casually suggested I dial down my daily dose of death metal, so clearly, we were having two entirely different conversations. She mentioned that sensorineural hearing loss patients often reported partial or full recovery over time, so there was hope, and I needn't sign up for an ASL or BANZSL crash course just yet. Like a good patient, I tried to follow all instructions with the hearing aid and underwent electrical ear canal stimulation to stave off the relentless tinnitus. But what no one ever tells you is how treatment itself can feel like a descent into a surreal abyss—a Greek myth version of the Infinite Void, where the noise becomes a sentient beast, each sound vying for attention, squeezing itself into the folds of my mind like a thousand frantic birds battering the gates of Tartarus.

Curiously, despite the cacophony, it wasn't entirely unbearable. The amplified world, though chaotic, came without the crushing migraines I'd feared. It was when the treatment actually started working—when the tinnitus quieted, and I dared to remove the hearing aid—that the real trouble began. The sheer silence was deafening, a void so impactful it made the noise seem like a merciful distraction. My brain, it seemed, had grown accustomed to the unrelenting clamor, and now, without it, panic set in. It's as if the sudden absence of sound left my mind scrambling, as though it had been anchored to the cacophony, and now, unmoored, it thrashed about, unable to ground itself.

And so, here it is, the research question: *How does the loss of a defining ability transform an individual's identity and perception? And further, how can synesthetic experiences in a gamified setting facilitate understanding and expression of this transformative experience?*

I'm asking this because, well, we probably need a research question that sounds suitably research-question-esque. But honestly, when the new normal of living without perfect pitch started sinking in, the real questions that haunted me were far more personal, far more existential.

Questions like: *Am I ... still me?* For those who knew me well, who had taken this so-called defining ability for granted—sometimes even more seriously than I did—how come they haven't disowned me? Why is no one panicking but me? And most importantly, how do I make peace with this new version of myself? How do I voice this transformation without unintentionally hurting myself all over again? I can't just hide out, waiting to magically return to *whole*—that's too pathetic, and besides, there's a solid chance I'll never be whole in the same way again. But pretending this never happened isn't an option either. It happened. It's real. And it's not going away.

* * *

I'd lost touch with Doraemon, theater chair, and the music engineer when my career took a different path, but some friendships never seem to need constant maintenance. They're just there. When I reached out to them, it was as if the last 20 years had evaporated. No awkward pauses or need to catch up on the highlights. We fell right into place, like a familiar chord. It was during one of these rekindled conversations that I shared my latest musings about the intersection of sound, art, and identity. They half-joking and half-serious, threw out the idea: If *Contours of Silence* was about tracing the "formless form," maybe you should design a game about "embracing the chaos." *Contours of Cacophony*. It was a clever turn of phrase—a challenge that sparked inspiration.

And just like that, the infinite journey took a new turn. Enter our Player One, *Bea*—a player referred by the music engineer from *Contours of Silence*. Once a virtuoso pianist, Bea had dazzled audiences with her mastery of the piano, but in recent years, recurring wrist pain forced her to step back from live performances. This physical limitation has not only affected her career but also her relationship with music itself. Now, Bea seeks to explore new ways of connecting with her artistry, hoping to reconcile her identity as a musician with the constraints imposed by her body. Piece by piece, the game design emerged. But before we get lost in the digital fantasy, let's anchor ourselves in the theoretical framework.

Theoretical Framework

To understand the transformation of identity following the loss of a defining ability, we must first ground our inquiry in phenomenology. Merleau-Ponty's (1962) exploration of perception and embodied experience offers crucial insight into how our sensory interactions shape self-awareness. Loss of a defining ability, therefore, is a disruption to one's phenomenological engagement with the world. It challenges the boundaries of the self, destabilizing the established relationship between body and environment. Recent works in phenomenological studies emphasize that sensory loss transforms the structure of lived experience (Gallagher, 2017). This transformation confronts individuals with the task of renegotiating their selfhood within a world that no longer feels familiar. Carel (2016) explored how illness and sensory impairments challenge our perceptions of self and force a renegotiation of our embodied experience. The relationship between bodily changes and selfhood enriches this exploration thus illustrated how the disruption of sensory experience prompts a reimagining of identity.

Existentialism also deepens this inquiry. In her work *The Ethics of Ambiguity*, de Beauvoir (1947) emphasizes the inherent tension between our freedom to transcend our circumstances and the reality of human finitude. The loss of perfect pitch, then, is not a final, fixed limitation but an opening to confront the paradox of my existence: while this loss constrains me, it also demands that I engage with my freedom to redefine what it means to listen, to communicate, and to exist in a newly configured world. De Beauvoir argues that meaning is found in actively confronting the contradictions of life, a process that reflects my journey through this altered soundscape. In addition, Frankl's (1984) concept of *tragic optimism* suggests that even in the face of suffering and loss, individuals can find meaning through resilience and a commitment to growth. Rather than signaling a collapse of identity, this new soundscape becomes an opportunity to engage with the world in new ways, crafting a narrative that embraces both limitation and possibility

However, identity does not transform in isolation; it is continuously reconstituted through narrative. *Narrative Identity Theory* (Ricoeur, 1992; McAdams, 2001) offers a framework for understanding how individuals re-story their lives in the wake of trauma or loss. Narrative of the players and the lorekeepers unfold dynamically within the game, where every choice represents a reconfiguration of their identity. Ricoeur's (1992) concept of "narrative time" suggests that our stories don't follow a linear path but are instead shaped by our capacity to reinterpret the past in light of the present. Meanwhile, *Disability Studies* complicates the reconstruction of identity by emphasizing the societal constructs that shape our understanding of ability and difference (Davis, 1995; Linton, 1998). The loss of a defining ability intersects with broader cultural narratives that frame deviations from normative ability as deviance. As individuals navigate this terrain, their identities are reshaped through the pressures and expectations imposed by society, which often stigmatizes difference. Such intersection echoes recent scholarship in disability theory that advocates for a reframing of disability from an individual deficit to an interplay between bodily variation and societal structures (Garland-Thomson, 2011). *Contours of Cacophony* thus becomes a synesthetic critique of the ways in which ability is socially constructed and navigated through gameplay, sound, and silence.

Conceptual Game Design: *Contours of Cacophony*

Game Setting: The game takes place in an expansive virtual theater, a symbolic space where both Bea, the player's past as a virtuoso pianist and myself, the Lorekeeper's auditory world collide. The theater is a performance space and a place of healing and reflection. It evolves dynamically, shifting between visual representations of music and the gradual silence that symbolizes Bea's physical limitations and the Lorekeeper's auditory challenges.

Gameplay Mechanics

Tactile Echoes: Throughout the theater, the player encounters tactile instruments that require gentle interaction. Each instrument requires finesse and caution due to her wrist pain, forcing her to rethink how she engages with the piano and other objects.

This reflects her struggle with her physical limitations, presenting a challenge that parallels her real-life experience with pain management.

Sensory Resonance Nodes: In this evolving space, the player also encounters glowing resonance nodes that bring both sound and touch into play. These nodes respond to both sound and light pressure, allowing Bea to explore music through careful, non-intrusive gestures. Each node reacts uniquely, sometimes fading out in response to her wrist pain, representing her need to adapt to new ways of interacting with her art.

Contours of Memories: As the player progresses, she relieves key memories of her musical career through fragmented auditory and tactile feedback. However, these memories are distorted, muffled, or incomplete, paralleling the Lorekeeper's partial hearing loss and the player's disconnection from the live performance world. The game setting invites the player to re-experience the joy of performance while also confronting the fragility of those moments, symbolized by the pain in her wrists.

Cacophony and Silence: Within certain chambers of the theater, Bea must play without relying on sound. Instead, vibrations and visual cues guide her actions. This silence echoes the Lorekeeper's partial hearing loss, challenging Bea to navigate the world without the usual auditory feedback. These silent sequences represent the symbiotic relationship between sound and touch, offering an introspective space for Bea to reflect on her journey.

Player Interaction

Adaptive Dialogue: The player's interaction with the environment and the Lorekeeper is deeply tied to their shared limitations. Instead of fast-paced dialogue, the game allows for slower, more contemplative exchanges. The dialogue trees adapt to her movements—If Bea's interactions become hesitant due to any physical or emotional discomfort, the Lorekeeper adjusts their responses, reflecting empathy and mutual understanding.

Synesthetic Puzzles: Bea faces puzzles that combine light, vibration, and tactile cues rather than sound. These puzzles require her to think creatively about how to solve challenges without relying on her past abilities, pushing her to forge new connections between senses.

Role of the Lorekeeper

The Lorekeeper, while guiding the player, also grapples with her own sensory limitation. This shared vulnerability shapes the interaction between the two. The Lorekeeper's responses change based on Bea's progress, reflecting an understanding of what it means to adapt to bodily constraints. They provide insight into both sound and silence, offering teach other wisdom from their own journey while co-creating a narrative that balances fragility, cacophony, and strength.

Environmental Shifts: The Lorekeeper can subtly shift the theater environment, guiding the player toward softer interactions with the space. Sometimes the theater becomes a hushed, almost soundless space to mirror the Lorekeeper's experience, while other times it fills with ambient vibrations that the player can feel through her fingertips rather than hear.

Objective: The goal of the game isn't to win or complete challenges in a traditional sense but to help Bea reimagine her relationship with music and her identity as a social member and an artist. The game becomes a metaphor for adapting to new limitations, creating a narrative of resilience and transformation. Bea's journey through the theater allows her to find new ways to express her artistry, while the Lorekeeper's guidance reflects their shared understanding of sensory loss and the need for creative adaptation.

Note: This conceptual game design envisions a highly immersive, adaptive environment. While current technology may not fully support all aspects of this design, the framework provides a speculative vision for how gaming can explore the intersections of sensory limitations and creative expression.

While the conceptual game design for *Contours of Cacophony* envisions a rich, immersive virtual environment that combines synesthetic experiences with tactile and auditory cues, current technological and resource limitations necessitate a more grounded approach. However, even without access to VR technology, we can maintain the essence of this narrative-driven experience, emphasizing creativity, adaptability, and participant agency. The following design offers a prototype that retains the core elements of the player's journey and the Lorekeeper's guiding presence. This approach allows us to explore the same themes—loss, adaptation, identity, and transformation—through more practical means, while still paving the way for a potential future iteration of the VR version.

Prototypical Game Design:
Contours of Cacophony

Setting
We anchor this version of the game in a physical space—a theater or auditorium balcony. The setting echoes the original concept's metaphorical stage, reinforcing the themes of performance, exploration, and reflection.

Auditorium Balcony: A relaxed, informal space that still embodies the performance and reflective aspects of the virtual theater. This allows the player to engage with the process in a more grounded, familiar environment, while still maintaining the thematic layers of the original concept.

Gameplay Mechanics
Index Cards as Dialogue Trees: In place of the immersive VR mechanics, we utilize index cards, each containing questions or prompts related to Bea's narrative and the *Contours of Cacophony* theme. The cards serve as a physical representation of the game's branching dialogue system.

The player can select cards at random or based on her intuition, mimicking the flexible, open-ended nature of the game.

The prompts vary in complexity, allowing her to control the depth of engagement, echoing the agency she would have in a virtual version.

Response Mechanism: After Bea responds to each card, new cards are introduced, gradually unlocking deeper layers of dialogue based on her previous responses. This mirrors the narrative progression in the VR version, where new layers of the game unfold as she moves forward.

Emotional and Thematic Mapping: Each card unlocks threads of Bea's story based on emotional responses or thematic continuity. For example, if Bea speaks of harmony, the next card might introduce discord, pushing her to explore contrasting emotions or ideas.

Documentation and Analysis

Recording Responses: With the player's consent, audio recordings can be made to capture her responses in detail. Alternatively, the Lorekeeper can take detailed notes, capturing both content and the nuances of Bea's emotional engagement.

Visual Mapping: A large visual map (either on paper or digitally) could be used to track the conversation's progression, representing the collaborative sound and silence from the conceptual design. This serves as a visual metaphor for the player's journey, mapping her emotions, ideas, and evolving relationship with her musical identity.

Index Cards as Dialogue Prompts

The index cards themselves are designed to encourage creativity and open dialogue, much like the environmental shift in the conceptual design. Examples include:

1. **Keyword: "Harmony"**
   (Invites the player to reflect on harmony, both in music and in her life or relationships, examining how her wrist injury has disrupted that balance.)

2. **Phrase: "Cacophonous Performance"**
   (Encourages the player to discuss moments when inharmonious cacophony has played a role in her identity as a musician, echoing the tactile-echo mechanic of the conceptual version.)

3. **Fill-in-the-Blank: "When my wrists decide to play *fortissimo*, the world feels like _____."**
   (opens up space for the player to explore her physical pain creatively, inviting her to consider the metaphorical impact it has on her world—whether it's loud and overpowering, or chaotic like an off-key symphony. It also keeps the tone light while still allowing for deep emotional exploration, as she describes her sensory or synesthetic experience of pain.)

4. **Multiple Choice: "The sound of chaos is ..." (Please elaborate.)**
   a) A kaleidoscope of overlapping melodies
   b) A conversation in an unfamiliar language
   c) A rainstorm that never quite hits the ground
   d) _____ (fills in your own interpretation, adding your personal experience of dissonance or confusion).

Logic to Unlock Next Narrative

Emotional Response Triggers: If the player expresses a strong emotional reaction to a particular card (e.g., frustration when discussing pain or joy when recalling a past performance), the next prompt can deepen that theme or introduce an emotional counterbalance.

Thematic Continuity: As themes like (in)harmony or silence emerge, follow-up prompts can introduce complementary or contrasting ideas, encouraging the player to explore the full spectrum of her experience.

Role of the Lorekeeper

The Lorekeeper maintains an active, empathetic presence, much like in the conceptual design, but instead of manipulating a virtual environment, she responds to the players' words and actions through conversation, guiding her through her journey while sharing their own experiences with partial hearing loss.

Mutual Storytelling: The dialogue between player and Lorekeeper evolves into a collaborative narrative, where both share stories of their respective limitations and adaptations. The Lorekeeper's auditory challenges serve as a reflective counterpoint to the player's now professional limitations, enriching the game's dialogue.

Objective: The goal remains the same: to co-create a narrative that helps the player navigate the complexities of her identity as a musician while acknowledging the limitations imposed by her wrist injury. The process becomes a dialogue-driven exploration, allowing the player to find new ways to express herself, not through victory or completion, but through understanding and transformation.

This prototypical version of *Contours of Cacophony* retains the core elements of the conceptual game design while making the experience feasible with existing resources. By combining creative prompts with a flexible narrative structure, it invites the player to explore her evolving relationship with music, identity, and physical limitations. The Lorekeeper's role, though grounded in a more feasible interaction, continues to foster a sense of mutual understanding and narrative co-creation. This approach ensures that, even without VR, the game still functions as a powerful tool for reflection, adaptation, and growth.

Contours of Identity: A Synesthetic Reflection

In the new reality where sound falters, and wrists tire,
Identity unfolds like a broken chord.
Not lost, but reshaped—
The self is rewritten, reconfigured through fragments of silence,
A synesthetic auditorium, where senses collide,
And limitations carve new paths toward becoming.

Merleau-Ponty whispers through the silence:
The body re-learns its world.
Touch replaces tone; the echo of effort replaces ease.
But here, in tactile resonance, the self awakens,
Learning not what is lost, but what is found
In every pause, every muted key.

Through *de Beauvoir's ambiguity*,
We transcend what constrains us—
Freedom dances in the gaps where sound once soared.
For in the void, meaning is not lost but born,
As wrists stiffen, the notes take new forms,
Felt in the interweaving of senses.

The game is no game at all—
But a space where sound becomes touch,
And silence becomes sound.
It is a journey, where the Lorekeeper leads not by hearing
But by feeling, through vibrations of shared limits,
Through whispers of possibility in the chaos of cacophony.

Ricoeur's narrative binds us:
Our stories do not end at loss.
They twist and turn through nodes of resonance,
Each memory a fragment of what was,
Each choice a re-construction of what could be.
Here, variations in ability is not deficit but transformation,
A new terrain of meaning, where cacophony is music,
And form takes shape from the formless void.

On the stage of this world,
Where limitations become the art itself,
Bea's hands may falter,
But her music—our music—continues to play
In the evolving contours of touch, sound, and silence,
StrataPlay unfolds—layer upon layer—
A cacophony of possibilities,
Where meaning rises from the spaces between.

Thus, the infinite journey continues ...

Player Two

Nourishing Legacies
Trauma, Motherhood, and Stuffed Grape Leaves

"Oh, now that's intriguing," I muttered, marking one index card *Stuffed grape leaves* with its sly little hint: *Tightly wrapped, yet filled with layers.* I slid it perfectly into place beside other culinary enigmas like *Fennel fronds* and *Cardamom pods.*

No, I haven't the faintest clue what these are—just like some of you, I suspect. I'm simply plucking random, intriguing sources as I enthusiastically craft a game for our Player Two, one that might just lift her spirits ever so slightly. (Or confuse her deeply. Either way, we're going for an experience.)

Now, for those of you curious souls, "Stuffed grape leaves are apparently a Middle Eastern and Mediterranean specialty—called *dolma* or *yaprak*, depending on the region." Think of them as little edible works of art: grape leaves meticulously wrapped around a filling of rice, herbs, and perhaps some meat. Culinary origami, really. Compact, complex, and layered, just like the hint promised.

As for the fennel fronds and cardamom pods? Google them yourselves. I've already blown my word count trying to sound like I know what I'm talking about, and I'd rather not waste any more on things that remain firmly outside my fridge and realm of expertise. It's not like I'm trying to impress you with my nonexistent culinary prowess—this isn't some random guest who automatically switches to mansplaining mode the moment they spot an unfamiliar spice.

The research question of the day is this:

> How can a gastronomy-centered, postqualitative game design facilitate the exploration of cross-generational trauma, identity reconstruction, and the nurturing role of motherhood, while integrating embodied metaphors of nourishment and care through creative gameplay?

(Yes, it's a mouthful. Let me break it down for you.)

The purpose of this inquiry is to delve into the complexities of motherhood and identity, using food as a lens for understanding how we inherit and transform trauma. By weaving gastronomy into game design, we create a space where nourishment is emotional, symbolic, and deeply intertwined with care and identity. Imagine a game where preparing a dish is an act of self-discovery, where each ingredient carries the weight of memory, and where cooking is a metaphor for reconstructing the self.

Cross-generational trauma refers to the invisible threads that bind one generation's pain to the next. As Marianne Hirsch (1997) discusses in her concept of *postmemory*, trauma often gets transmitted from parent to child not through direct experience but through inherited memories, which shape the emotions of the next generation. This trauma is an unspoken inheritance passed down from mother to daughter, often without either party realizing it's happening. As Cathy Caruth (1996) argues, trauma is something that echoes across generations, residing in the stories that remain untold and the emotions left unprocessed. These silences, as Nicolas Abraham and Maria Torok (1994) describe in their theory of the "phantom," live in the suppressed emotions and the patterns repeated within families, haunting descendants without their explicit awareness. Trauma may also be passed down through cultural and racial lines. As Anne Anlin Cheng (2001) suggests in *The Melancholy of Race*, unspoken grief can become embedded in familial and cultural identities, shaping how subsequent generations understand their place in the world. Similarly, Sara Ahmed (2004) emphasizes the importance of emotion in familial and cultural narratives, explaining how feelings such as grief and anger move between bodies, affecting collective experiences. The unaddressed trauma and emotional repression create patterns that can be passed down through generations, perpetuating cycles of unspoken pain. Through food, however, we can begin to unravel those threads. Ingredients, after all, are passed down too—recipes, methods, rituals. They represent a way to either perpetuate or break free from the past.

Motherhood, at its core, is about nurturing—but it's also about identity. As Ruddick (1989) suggests in *Maternal Thinking*, mothering is a practice that involves the continuous balancing of care, emotional labor, and identity formation. A mother nourishes not only with food but with love and the relentless care that defines the role. Yet, the act of mothering often forces a renegotiation of one's own sense of self. Who am I, apart from my child? Adrienne Rich (1986), in *Of Woman Born*, discusses the tension between motherhood as an institution and as an experience, exploring how societal expectations can often challenge the personal identity of mothers. Food, in this context, becomes a metaphor for the push and pull of motherhood—balancing flavors, adding, subtracting, and continuously striving for a *perfect recipe* that simply doesn't exist (Ruddick, 1989). Meanwhile, nourishment is, as Carolyn Korsmeyer (1999) suggests in *Making Sense of Taste*, an embodied metaphor for care—care of the self, care of others, and care of the legacies we leave behind. By centering nourishment in this postqualitative game design, we can explore the emotional labor of feeding others while examining the broader implications of what it means to nourish a family, a lineage, and a self through acts of creation. This echoes Bachelard's (1964) notion in *The Poetics of Space*, where the kitchen and acts of feeding become symbolically linked to nurturing both body and soul, blending nourishment with emotional and creative care. In short, this round of gameplay is about using the art of cooking as a tool for storytelling—a way to digest, quite literally, the traumas and triumphs that shape who we are.

Index Cards for Player Two: Nourishing Legacies

1. *Quinoa*
   (Tiny but packed with power—hidden strengths in small things)

2. *Green apples*
   (Tart and crisp—biting through fresh beginnings)

3. *Seaweed*
   (Rooted in water—resilience in ever-changing environments)

4. *Truffle oil*
   (Rich and earthy—luxury from beneath the surface)

5. *Bitter melon*
   (Bitter with a hint of warmth)

6. *Bone broth*
   (Boiled for hours—what do you need to extract with patience?)

7. *Chia seeds*
   (Tiny seeds that expand—potential waiting to grow)

8. *Trout*
   (Swimming through familiar waters)

9. *Roasted beetroot*
   (Deep roots with new growth)

10. *Chestnuts*
    (A hard shell but soft inside—what takes time to open up?)

11. *Tagliatelle*
    (Intertwined, complex threads)

12. *Duck confit*
    (Preserved through slow cooking—what endures long-term care?)

13. *Star anise*
    (A star-shaped spice—guidance or direction?)

14. *Lemon and rosemary sorbet*
    (A fresh start)

15. *Braised lamb*
    (Tender care and slow growth)

16. *Assorted cheeses*
    (Rich and varied—sharp at times)

17. *Chocolate tart with chili*
    (Sweetness with a surprise kick)

18. *Layered cake*
    (Layered and chaotic, yet delightful)

19. *Persimmons*
    (Sweet only after ripening—what comes with waiting?)

20. *Herbal tea*
    (Soothing with depth)

21. *Saffron threads*
    (Rare and delicate—flavor drawn from patience)

22. *Black garlic*
    (Aged to sweetness—what gets better with time?)

23. *Anchovies*
    (Salty and bold—an acquired taste?)

24. *Pickled cucumber*
    (An intense flavor from the past)

25. *Stuffed grape leaves*
    (Tightly wrapped, yet filled with layers)

26. *Smoked paprika*
    (Earthy and intense—what lingers after the fire?)

> 27. *Avocado*
>   (Smooth yet fragile—what easily bruises but nourishes deeply?)
>
> 28. *Cardamom pods*
>   (Small but fragrant—what's hidden within?)
>
> 29. *Pomegranate seeds*
>   (Bright and bursting—what's locked inside your armor?)
>
> 30. *Cilantro*
>   (Divisive but essential—what flavors do you love or hate?)
>
> 31. *Red wine reduction*
>   (Deep and concentrated—what becomes richer through loss?)
>
> 32. *Fennel fronds*
>   (Feathery but strong—lightness with a solid foundation)

Nana narrowed her eyes suspiciously as she sifted through the so-called index-card-bound *ingredients*.

"I knew something's off when you said it would be a game, and that we'd cook together at your place, and all I had to bring was myself. I should've seen it coming. You can't cook! How could I have expected you to prepare proper, *real* ingredients?" she grumbled, eyeing the cards with the skepticism of a seasoned connoisseur.

"Well, technically I can cook. I just ... most of the time choose not to," I countered, trying to sound confident but knowing full well where this conversation was headed. "It's just, by the time I'm done cooking, I've lost my appetite, and then it takes forever to clean up. I'd rather spend that time crafting a poem or something."

Nana raised an eyebrow. "So, no ingredients, and now poetry?"

"It's not like I'm going to let you starve!" I protested, digging through the paper bag. "I ordered us Happy Meals. Sanrio toys are in the mix. If we're lucky, one of us might even score a *Kuromi* today!" I tried to keep a straight face. Then, with a formal tone, I added, "Please note that you are free to withdraw from this game at any time, without penalty or consequence to you. Your participation is entirely voluntary, and should you choose to discontinue at any point, you are under no obligation to complete the activity. The only potential loss might be sharing a Happy Meal with me, but rest assured, no further repercussions will follow."

Prototypical Game Design: Nourishing Legacies

Game Setting
The game is set in a kitchen, a symbolic space where nurturing, memory, and trauma intersect. This intimate environment serves as a backdrop for the player's emotional and personal journey. Each culinary creation thus becomes a metaphor for exploring her identity, the complex relationship with her daughter, and the weight of cross-generational expectations that she carries. The kitchen is where nourishment, both literal and metaphorical, takes place.

Gameplay Mechanics
Index Cards as Ingredients. The 32 index cards represent metaphorical ingredients. Each card is selected to form part of a 12-course meal, but beyond that, it triggers a memory, reflection, or decision tied to the player's personal journey and identity as a mother. Each ingredient becomes a tool for reflection—perhaps an "ingredient" from her past, a tradition passed down, or an emotion that needs processing.

Culinary Synesthesia. Much like the synesthetic experiences in *Contours of Cacophony*, each ingredient card is designed to evoke a culinary memory that ties into the senses, sparking a sensory memory, an emotion, or a reflection on motherhood and identity. The player might smell the scent of a dish, only to be reminded of her grandmother's kitchen, or taste something that takes her back to a pivotal moment in her life. These sensory experiences are woven into the game, creating deeper layers of meaning.

12-Course Menu Construction

As the player progresses through the game, she constructs a metaphorical 12-course menu. Each course represents a stage in her emotional evolution—perhaps balancing the sweetness of her child's love with the bitterness of inherited trauma, or the complexity of blending her cultural heritage with her own personal values. The final menu thus becomes a story of motherhood, resilience, and transformation.

The Role of the Lorekeeper

The Lorekeeper plays an essential role, gently guiding the player through each culinary decision. By listening to the player's reflections, the Lorekeeper helps her draw connections between food, memory, and identity, highlighting how the act of cooking mirrors the emotional labor of caregiving.

With thoughtful prompts, the Lorekeeper helps clarify the metaphors embedded in the index cards, encouraging the player to reflect on how time, experience, and motherhood have shaped her perspective. The Lorekeeper's role is not to lead but to facilitate—acting as both a co-creator of the narrative and a reflective mirror.

And, on a practical note, the Lorekeeper must order McDonald's to keep the mood light, and if a Kuromi toy does happen to grace the Happy Meal, it must be secured—no compromises.

"I've got to hand it to you—for someone who can't cook, you've got a bizarrely refined taste in index cards," Nana ribbed, plucking out cards as if she were assembling a Michelin-star menu from a pile of laminated paper. She was already halfway through constructing her ideal 12-course dinner.

"I *can* cook. I just ... don't," I muttered, clinging to the last scraps of dignity I had left.

"*Star anise,*" she chuckled, holding the card up. "I'm surprised you even know what that is."

"I mean, I've never actually used it," I recalled, "but my dad used to toss star anise into his braised pork stew—said it helped cut through the gaminess of the meat while adding a subtle layer of warmth and sweetness. The aromatics from the star anise balance out the richness, leaving a deeper, more nuanced flavor."

"Ah, of course. You're pretty much Gordon Ramsay in theory," she quipped, her eyes lingering for just a second too long on an old stain on the wall behind me.

I sighed. "Look, I know that stain looks ... suspicious, but it's not what you think. That's a Mentos and Coke experiment gone wrong, courtesy of my 8-year-old roommate. I just haven't had a chance to repaint it yet."

Nana waved me off casually. "Oh, no, I wasn't thinking that. I know it's not blood. When my mom beat me years ago, blood always got on the walls—it leaves uneven stains, you know? Some patches turn out lighter, some darker. And after a while, they turn black, not that light coffee color."

I swallowed, "Girl, you just said something deeply disturbing with the calmness of someone describing a weather report."

She just smiled, letting the moment hang in the air.

I cleared my throat. "So, what've you got there?" I peeked at her stack of cards, curious about how she'd handle the fish course and main. My attention snagged on the *Stuffed Grape Leaves* card sitting comfortably in her "to be used" pile. "I only threw that in there to mess with you," I admitted. "I had no idea what it even was until I looked it up."

Nana shrugged casually. "It's like *Chimaki*. Your hint down here is interesting, though." She pointed to the note I'd scribbled: *Tightly wrapped, yet filled with layers.* "I think it'd make a solid appetizer—with lemon and dill for some sharpness."

"What are you going to name it?" I asked, keeping my tone light.

" ... 'Weight,' maybe?" She paused. "No, wait. *The Burden of Tradition.*"

"Burden," I echoed, rolling the word around.

"Some inherited traditions feel heavy, don't you think?" She said it like it was an afterthought. "For so long, I thought I had to carry that weight. Like if I didn't, I'd be breaking some unwritten rule of filial piety—betraying everything I came from by daring to find my own meaning. And that's why I never wanted a kid. I didn't want to pass that weight down to another generation."

I nodded, trying to ask lightly. "But ... do you regret it? Having a child after all?"

"Regret?" Nana chuckled softly. "No, not at all. Honestly, I barely remember how I survived before she came into my life."

Nana's past had been rough—her childhood marked by abuse, the kind of trauma that stays like an unwelcome houseguest. Now she was raising her daughter on her own while juggling life as a full-time middle school teacher. I met her once while subbing at her school, filling in for a friend. She had this aura, something unspoken, and I just knew she had Japanese roots. One conversation led to another, and somehow, she agreed to be part of this suspicious project of mine.

I pointed to another card sitting curiously in her "to be used" pile, one I'd avoid at all costs: *Bitter melon.*

"What's the grand plan for something that literally has 'bitter' in its name?" I chuckled.

"Oh, it's for the soup. Bitter melon and ginger broth. I've got a good title for this one," she nodded, with a seriousness that made me nervous.

I had a bad feeling about this.

"It's for your own good," she announced.

I cringed. "I'd rather not. I've heard it's good for you—lowers blood pressure or blood sugar or something. But I'm definitely not masochistic enough to enjoy bitter cuisine."

"No," she corrected, *"It's for your own good"*—that's the title. The soup course is called "It's for your own good."

" ... Fine," I conceded.

"But it really does lower your blood sugar. You should eat more of it, considering you've had gestational diabetes. Did your PCP not warn you that puts you at a higher risk for type II diabetes?" She sounded like a seasoned salesperson—one who'd mastered the art of peddling bitter melon. "Here," she said, sliding the index card toward me, "take it. 'It's for your own good'."

I thank you very much.

> **Disclaimer:** *I take no responsibility for any unsolicited health advice given by our players during gameplay. Please consult actual medical or nutrition professionals for legitimate advice regarding the effects of bitter melons.*

Shifting gears, I asked, "Got a good title for your main?" I glanced at her as she studied her *Braised Lamb* card, its footnote dripping with cheesiness thanks to yours truly: *Tender care and slow growth.*

She grinned. "I'm thinking 'Love You Three Thousand,' but I'm not sure if Marvel's going to come for me."

I smirked. "You could make it a little less cheesy and more original, you know."

She paused, thinking for a moment. "Alright, scratch 'Love You Three Thousand.' Let's go with 'Slow Burn.' It's about something that doesn't blaze up all at once but stays steady and warm, lasting through time. Like how you don't rush anything. You let it simmer, because that's how it deepens."

I shot her a side-eye. "Are we still talking about food ... ? Or something that's on top of my mind, dangerously close to veering down the wrong aisle?"

She didn't miss a beat. "I don't know. You tell me. Have we *ever* really been talking about food since the beginning?"

Without waiting for my answer, she slid her next card toward me. "Pan-seared trout with saffron and fennel—fish course. I propose we call it 'Waters of Change.'"

I nodded. The title worked magically. It reminded me of the fluidity of identity, the effort it takes to craft something new from the familiar waters of one's past. And the watery imagery stirred up a memory of a friend who, expecting her first child, often mused about how she felt more and more like liquid—*a woman of water*. She was full of it, from the womb to the bladder, to the tears that welled in her eyes. Soon, she would flow from her chest, a fountain of joy, of worry, and nourishment—an ever-flowing current of life itself.

"I think I'm done putting together that 12-course you requested," she said, proudly presenting her impromptu yet beautifully arranged menu.

12-Course Menu: Nourishing Legacies

1. Amuse-Bouche: Diluted Heritage
   (Pickled cucumber with mint and yogurt)
   From vine to jar, the sharpness fades,
   A bitterness tamed for gentler ways.
   I soften the past with each passing year,
   Diluting its bite, so you, my dearest daughter, need not fear.

2. Appetizer: The Burden of Tradition
   (Stuffed grape leaves with lemon and dill)
   Wrapped tight like the stories we bear,
   Heavy, delicate, seasoned with care.
   Traditions fold in, flavors unfold,
   A burden passed down, bitter and bold.

3. Soup: "For Your Own Good"
   (Bitter melon and ginger broth)
   "It's for your own good," they'd yell from the door,
   Bitter words, like the soup they'd pour.
   Sharp on the tongue, yet ginger's embrace,
   A warmth that lingers, chasing the taste.

4. Fish Course: Waters of Change
   (Pan-seared trout with saffron and fennel)
   Saffron's bright glow, fennel's soft breeze,
   I rebuild myself in waters like these.

5. Salad: Roots and Shoots
   (Roasted beetroot and arugula salad with pomegranate dressing)
   Roots dig deep,
   Shoots reach out,
   Generations clash, yet tenderly grow,
   A salad of past, present, future, all in tow.

6. Pasta: Entangled
   (Homemade tagliatelle with roasted tomato and basil)
   Past and present, futures unknown.

Each strand a thread, woven with care,
Stories of love, loss, whispered in air.

7. Intermezzo: Cleansing the Past
   (Lemon and rosemary sorbet)
   A cool breeze, a cleansing sip,
   The past melts away, refreshing the soul.

8. Main Course: Slow Burn
   (Braised lamb with thyme and honey glaze)
   The fire's low, the sweetness seeps,
   Through tender meat, where patience keeps.
   Honey's warmth softens the pain,
   My love to you, slow, but never in vain.

9. Cheese Course: Complexity of Care
   (Assorted cheeses with figs and walnuts)
   Care is layered.
   Tangled moments, incomplete.
   A balance of flavors, bold and mild,
   The complexity of nurturing.

10. Pre-Dessert: Sweet Resilience
    (Mini chocolate tart with chili pepper)
    Sweet melts on the tongue,
    Hidden heat sparks in the dark—
    Strength wrapped in silence.

11. Dessert: Messy Love
    (Layered cake with raspberry, chocolate, and cream)
    Love crumbles and soars,
    Layers of chaos and peace.
    Sweet, bitter, untamed.

12. Digestif: The Future Brewed
    (Herbal tea with lavender, chamomile, and mint)
    Lavender's dream, chamomile's peace,
    A quiet promise.

As Nana concluded her final card, I couldn't help but admire the journey we'd just completed—a journey of banter, flavors, memories, and metaphors, wrapped in the comforting and chaotic language of food. What began as a playful experiment, an excuse to build something out of index cards and conversation, evolved into something far more meaningful with each dish. Through this gastronomy-centered, unconventional game design, Nana and I navigated the layered terrain of cross-generational trauma and identity reconstruction. The *Bitter melon and ginger broth* reminded us of the uncomfortable truths often delivered under the guise of care. The *Stuffed grape leaves* and their "burden of tradition" captured the weight of what we inherit. And yet, the *Braised lamb* in "Slow Burn" showed us that with time and patience, even the most bitter roots can give way to sweetness, symbolizing the evolving love between mother and child. The kitchen became our stage, where the act of selecting ingredients transformed into a dialogue about past and present, a conversation between trauma and resilience. With each course, the player was reconstructing herself, healing those invisible wounds left by past generations, and reimagining what motherhood could be.

Ultimately, the research question—*How can a gastronomy-centered, postqualitative game design facilitate the exploration of cross-generational trauma, identity reconstruction, and the nurturing role of motherhood?*—found its tentative answer here, in this kitchen, between lighthearted banter, bittersweet memories, and the slow, intentional work of reimagining what it means to care. Through the metaphors of food and culinary practice, we re-encounter the tensions of identity and legacy. In this kitchen, the labor of love manifests in the emotional work of balancing tradition and autonomy (Ruddick, 1989). The ways Nana processes the inherited burdens of her postmemory (Hirsch, 1997) demonstrate the power of embodied metaphors (*Bitter melon* and *Stuffed grape leaves*) in unraveling trauma that is deeply *felt*. These emotional and sensory experiences facilitate the reconstruction of Nana's identity in the context of motherhood, showing how she can carve out new spaces of care, free from the shackles of inherited pain.

This game design serves as a mode of inquiry, aligned with St. Pierre's (2011) concept of postqualitative approach that resists traditional linear narratives and embraces complexity, uncertainty, and the transformative potential of creative exploration. The kitchen as a site of play allows for a *nomadic subjectivity* (Braidotti, 1994), where Nana moves between inherited identities and self-creation, constructing herself through layers of emotion, mirroring the dishes she creates. In this way, *Nourishing Legacies* embodies a fluid, dynamic form of inquiry, where trauma, care, and identity can be explored beyond static interviews or surveys. Through embodied metaphors of food, we unearthed her side of the stories into the nurturing role of motherhood, uncovering the strength, resilience, and creativity required to sustain, to heal, and to transform life.

Almost forgot.

Just in case you're wondering—though I suspect not many of you are, and fewer still actually care—I'm going to share anyway. Turns out neither of our Happy Meals came with the Kuromi toy. I know, a real tragedy. And here's the kicker: we both got Melody. Of all the characters, the sweet, innocent, goody-two-shoes Melody. Not even a hint of chaos in sight. So, there you have it, a real tragedy.

Player Three

TnT the Word RPG
Neal Libertas and the Post-Edu Apocalypse

"I exist in Thoughtspire, though I cannot say why. Nor can I say for how long."

"In a place where beginnings and endings blur, I am both the traveler and the lost. This is not a maze of walls but of words—definitions twisting upon themselves until even the word 'meaning' loses its meaning."

"Somewhere, a paper-cut festers. A wound no one asked for, inflicted by bureaucracy, sharpened by the edges of an abstract longer than 350 words that was never read. I am to find it, though no one told me why. This is the task assigned to me, and so I accept it, for what is existence but the relentless acceptance of the absurd? Like Sisyphus pushing his boulder, I, too, must roll my questions up a hill, only to watch them tumble down the other side—answered by no one."

"Neoliberalism breathes down my neck, whispering of 'productivity' and 'deliverables,' though I suspect these are all synonyms for absurdity. The corridors of Thoughtspire twist in impossible angles, not by anime logic but by the logic of thought itself—a Beckettian farce where nothing ever arrives and everything is perpetually flowing."

"I am the Dung Beetle, now—whether by choice or by accident, I can no longer tell. I push my ball of absurdity through these winding corridors, searching for the paper cut. Or is it searching for me? They were right; we wait. We always wait."

" ... We always wait ... wait ... wait ... " I echoed my last line, drawing it out with an unnecessary, but highly satisfying, manual reverb.

All three of them—our players—stared back at me, the collective thought bubble, *"She's finally lost it"* practically hovering above their heads like a danmaku.

Yes, *Player Three* was, in fact, three players. All former students from my writing-emphasis course, bless their souls. And now, inexplicably, all caught in the tangled web of education. Bless their souls again.

"Welcome," I said, raising my hands with the flourish of a seasoned Dungeon Master ... ahem, Lorekeeper. "Welcome to *Thoughtspire and Tales*, or *TnT* for short. No relation to *DnD*, I assure you. My name is Mila Troubleclef, your absurdly devoted Lorekeeper for this journey into the unknown vortex of post-educational calamity."

I paused, letting the moment breathe.

"Now that you've all been helplessly sucked into this interdimensional labyrinth of paradoxes, I will guide you—whether you like it or not. Together, we shall conquer the utterly absurd challenges placed before us. We will craft our saga, a tale that no one asked for, nor will they care about ... and neither, I might add, were these challenges even necessary in the first place."

They blinked. And blinked once more for good measure.

"I have ... so many questions," one of them finally said, managing to string together the words.

"I'm sure you do, Beckett," I acknowledged him with the resigned patience of an educator.

"And now I have another question—who's Beckett?" He seized the chance, a burning question finally escaping his lips.

"You," I said, as if explaining something perfectly obvious, "in *Thoughtspire*, today, you're donning the avatar of one Beckett."

I gestured grandly, as if bestowing upon him some mythical title, all the while maintaining the patience of a high school math teacher. "And you, my dear," I turned to the second player, "are Juliet."

"Sure." Juliet accepted her fate enthusiastically.

Beckett turned to her, eyebrows raised, with an expression that translated only too clearly into a look that said, ... *really?*

The third player, not wanting to be left out of the confusion, finally chimed in. "What about me?"

"Ah, yes." I nodded sagely. "You are Player IX."

A pause.

"Okay, why do I sound like I'm in a completely different anime system?" He shot back, his tone laced with the kind of rebellion that reminded me of students with a chronic knack for challenging authority.

"Because 'Player X' reads confusing." I replied, my voice still dripping with saint-like patience. "How do you know our future readers won't peg the 'X' in your name as a letter, as opposed to a number?"

"I know you're trying to answer my question … but maybe try harder." He looked unimpressed.

"Great!" I clapped my hands, completely undeterred. "Now that we're all crystal clear, let's embrace our very first challenge."

Magical-Post-Realism: A New Lens in the Post-Presence Epoch

Thoughtspire, the labyrinth at the heart of *TnT* (*Thoughtspire and Tales*), is an interdimensional maze where reality bends under the weight of language, culture, and absurdity. It's a place where logic has been left at the door, and the only way forward is through storytelling—a skill our players will need to survive.

TnT is a word RPG (role-playing game), a collaborative storytelling experience where both player and Lorekeeper—your humble guide—craft a narrative together. Instead of rolling dice or performing action-based moves, players use words and dialogues to navigate challenges, with each decision shaping the journey. Here, in *Thoughtspire*, absurdity reigns. Language and culture are lost in translation, while players tackle impossible tasks in a space in between dimensions that mirrors the paradoxes of academia.

The research question that has prompted the design of TnT is: *How can an absurd word RPG, set in a post-educational labyrinth, facilitate critical reflection on the intersection of culture, paradoxes, and neoliberalism inherent in academia?*

In the design of TnT, I propose the theory of *Magical-Post-Realism*, a framework that blends the fantastical with the mundane, grounded in the peculiarities of contemporary life—especially in the Post-Presence Epoch of Zoom fatigue, digital fragmentation, and neoliberal absurdity. At its core, Magical-Post-Realism exists at the intersection of magical realism, postmodernism, posthumanism, and absurdism, as it reflects both lived experiences and their surreal amplification in academia.

Magical Realism as a Foundation. Magical-Post-Realism draws from the tradition of magical realism, a literary genre where the extraordinary is woven seamlessly into the everyday. Magical realism, as seen in the works of García Márquez and Allende, does not question the presence of the supernatural; it exists alongside reality, often as a commentary on social and cultural structures (Faris, 2004). Similarly, Magical-Post-Realism in this gameplay uses the fantastical elements of *TnT*—such as talking dung beetles and mythical creatures like "Neal Libertas"—as metaphors for real-world struggles in academia.

Postmodernism and Hyperreality. Building on Jean Baudrillard's (1983) concept of "simulacra," Magical-Post-Realism also interrogates the notion of reality itself. In *TnT*, reality is warped and refracted through language, creating a postmodern terrain where players' experiences are no longer directly connected to the real, but to representations and distortions of it. The term *Post Presence Epoch*, introduced in the chapter of "Game Start," reflects this dissonance—where participants are simultaneously present in virtual spaces but not truly present in a traditional sense. The labyrinth of *Thoughtspire* mirrors this disconnection, as players navigate a space where meaning is fluid and existence is simultaneously real and abstract.

Posthumanism and Identity. The theory of Magical Post-Realism blends elements of magical realism with posthuman and post-realist thinking, reflecting the complexities of our technologically mediated, socially fractured era. This concept resonates deeply with Haraway's "Chthulucene" and Braidotti's "posthumanist subjectivity," where traditional boundaries between human and non-human, real and virtual, collapse. Haraway's (2016) discussion of the "Chthulucene" challenges the dominance of the Anthropocene, advocating for a relational ontology that intertwines human, non-human, and technological agents, moving away from anthropocentrism toward a vision of multispecies flourishing. The notion of "becoming-with" suggests that identity is not fixed but constantly shaped through relationships with the world, including both organic and technological entities. Such positionality aligns with our *post-real* world in which virtual and absurd realities blur with lived experiences.

In her speech, *Posthuman, All Too Human*, Braidotti (2017) argues that the posthuman subject is materially embedded and relational, rejecting both humanism and anthropocentrism. She explores how technological advances and ecological crises compel us to reconsider what it means to be human. This posthuman perspective reinforces the notion that Magical Post-Realism is both an escapist fantasy and an exploration of how absurdity, technology, and identity are intertwined in a constantly shifting multiverse. In the context of Thoughtspire and TnT, Magical Post-Realism becomes a tool to critique neoliberal academia while inviting players to navigate a labyrinth of paradoxes and contradictions. The blending of real-life struggles, such as academic absurdities and personal trauma, with fantastical and surreal challenges reflects the posthuman subject's constant negotiation of identity and reality, deeply influenced by material and non-human forces. Such juxtaposition allows for critical reflection on how identity is shaped by external structures—be they institutional, societal, or even metaphysical. By embedding Magical Post-Realism in the gameplay, players are invited to navigate the complexities the Post-Presence Epoch. Such metaphorical immersion evokes both the philosophical absurdity of Camus (1942) and the performative nonsense of Beckett (1953), where meaning is constantly deferred, and yet, the players persist.

Absurdism and the Search for Meaning. Magical-Post-Realism is deeply informed by Albert Camus' (1942) philosophy of the absurd, where individuals search for meaning in a world that offers none. In *TnT*, the absurdity is not merely for humor but serves as a critical lens through which the players confront the contradictions of academia. The challenges—such as teaching 0 students—mirror real frustrations within the academic system, particularly under neoliberal conditions where productivity and success are often detached from meaningful outcomes. The endless pursuit of marketability and efficiency in the labyrinth is reflective of the Sisyphean struggle to find meaning in an increasingly absurd allegory.

* * *

Challenge One: The Post-Edu Apocalyptic Faculty Meeting

In the beginning, it was not chaos, nor the fire and brimstone so often prophesied.

The world of academia didn't collapse all at once—it quietly unraveled. The signs were subtle at first: students fading away from their Zoom screens, syllabi left unread, the campus ghostly silent. The great halls of learning—temples built to house knowledge—now stood empty, mere husks of their former grandeur. The libraries became tombs for unread research studies and untouched archives. No angry protests. No riots. Just a slow fade into nothingness, as if reality itself had grown bored with the effort of higher education and decided to move on without us.

The classrooms turned into voids, echoing with the absence of those who once filled them. Even the grading software crashed, as though refusing to acknowledge assignments that would never be submitted. One by one, the systems failed—not with a bang, but with the soft hum of servers powering down. And now, you remain—faculty, in name only.

The Lorekeeper clears her throat, her voice echoing with the gravity of a dark prophecy.

You look around.

"Enrollment has hit zero," the Lorekeeper continues. "And yet, even in this apocalypse, your task remains clear: provide *world-class education*. For whom? No one. But your mission, noble educators, remains ... unchanged."

The "agenda" appears in front of the players, projected onto a faded whiteboard:

- *0 assignments,*
- *0 course credits,*
- *student loan cancellation (with 0 loans to cancel),*
- *Travel to conferences on a budget of $0,*
- *Complete professional development on successfully teaching 0 students.*

Beckett is the first to speak, his voice deadpan and emotionless. "I'm just saying … how do you cancel a loan that doesn't exist?" He gestures vaguely, as if the rest of the agenda items all make perfect sense.

Juliet raises a finger. "Actually, zero *is* the loan. The loan amount is exactly zero. It's the ultimate in student debt forgiveness. They owe nothing, but that nothing is now forgiven in perpetuity."

Beckett stares at her, "Really now?!"

Juliet shrugs. "Hey, she decided the premise. I just … interpret the zeros."

Player IX chimes in. "But 0 assignments, 0 credits? Sounds like a fantastic marketing strategy, really." His eyes light up. "Imagine it—guaranteed success. We'll promise to attract just 0 more students! All zero of you are A+ material! No assignments, no work, no stress—just pure, unadulterated success." He pauses, letting the brilliance of his strategic thinking sink in, "We could call it *The Ultimate Education Experience* … and guarantee absolutely *nothing*."

The Lorekeeper smiles at *you* enigmatically. "And so it begins, the great paradox of the post-education apocalypse. Your task is not to find meaning … but to exist in it, where none exists."

* * *

Challenge Two: Neal Libertas: An Autobiography

Neal Libertas wasn't born in a blaze of fire or from the depths of some dark forest. No, he was born in the sterile, whitewashed boardrooms of policymakers who saw education not as a public good but as an investment. His first breath was taken when schools were told they were no longer sacred places of learning, but businesses, subject to the cold logic of profit margins and "efficiency." Libertas thrived in the era of New Public Management, where institutions of higher education were required to function like corporations, maximizing outputs while minimizing costs. He roamed across campuses, devouring faculty autonomy, turning students into customers and education into a product (Ball, 2016). His diet consisted of "accountability measures" and "standardized testing," growing larger and more grotesque with every underfunded public school and each contingent faculty contract (Ingleby, 2021).

Neal's true strength lies in his ability to convince institutions that they must compete against one another, where success is measured not by the richness of knowledge

> or the development of critical thought, but by graduation rates, student satisfaction surveys, and employability statistics (Savage, 2017). He loves performance-based funding, which ensures the rich schools get richer, while underperforming schools—his favorite snacks—are starved of resources (Gray et al., 2018). In Libertas's world, "student debt" isn't a problem; it's a "product." He knows how to market education like a fast-food menu, offering an array of degrees with no guarantee of a future, while universities continue to churn out more students into an already saturated labor market. For every dropout, every underemployed graduate, Neal grows stronger.
>
> Now, in the post-edu apocalypse, Neal Libertas wanders the halls of empty campuses. His whispers echo through the decrepit faculty lounges, promising efficiency, market reform, and freedom—though his "freedom" comes at the cost of everything else ...

The Lorekeeper clears her throat, adopting an expression of utmost seriousness. "And so, the saga of *Neal Libertas*, devourer of underperforming campuses and destroyer of the public good, unfolds. In this round of the challenge, your task is to retell the brief history of Neal, but you must cater to various readerships. For example, Kuromi fans—lovers of the adorable yet mischievous."

Juliet interrupts with a flourish. "Oh no, no. We simply *must* have a Regency novel edition of this tale. Something with Mr. Libertas, dashing yet sinister, ruining campuses with the politest of manners."

Beckett raises an eyebrow. "Please. We can't stop at Regency. We need a Shakespearean edition. The fall of universities as a tragic drama of betrayal and hubris. Think of the soliloquies."

Player IX leans forward, grinning. "Forget that old-school stuff. We need a Gen Alpha edition—meme culture, TikToks, everything quick, loud, and straight to the point."

Neal Libertas: An Autobiography

Gen Alpha Edition
By: The Players
Logged by the Lorekeeper

Yo fam, it's ya boi Neal Libertas. You've probably seen me on TikTok, blowing up schools (don't @ me), and snacking on underperforming teachers like they're yesterday's trends. I've been out here doing my thing, disrupting the *edu* game since day one.

Listen up, because I know you're about that short attention span life, so I'mma make this fast. Picture this: education is like that game you used to play before Fortnite—totally irrelevant now. That's where I come in. I'm here to shake things up, give you the freedom to YOLO your way through academia. No grades? No problem. You know what's better than homework? No homework. I got you, fam.

My Origin Story. Back in the day, schools were like, "Let's teach kids stuff that matters," and I was like, "Nah, let's turn this into a capitalist playground." Now, instead of learning, you're swiping through tests like Tinder profiles. Swipe left for critical thinking, swipe right for standardized tests. It's all about metrics, baby—likes, shares, and that sweet GPA drip.

Oh, and if you're wondering how I survive, it's easy. I feed off the collapse of *engagement*. No likes? No funding. No funding? School's gone. *Yeet.*

My Vibe Check. I don't teach. I disrupt. You don't learn; you vibe. The old heads wanted students to succeed or whatever, but I knew better. Success is just one more TikTok away. Now schools are like, "Teach 0 students, give 0 assignments," and I'm here for it. What's the point of teaching when I can just drop a viral hashtag and call it a day?

So yeah, if you're looking for *real* education, you're in the wrong era. But if you're about that *influencer life*—welcome to my world, Gen Alpha. Like, share, and subscribe to my vibe.

#StayWoke #EatSchools #NoHomeworkLife

End Transmission by the Lorekeeper. "Neal's logic is flawless—assuming you were expecting absolutely none to begin with."

Neal Libertas: An Autobiography

Regency Novel Edition
By: The Players
Logged and edited (with impeccable manners) by the Lorekeeper

It is a truth universally acknowledged, that a single man in possession of a large estate must, indeed, be in want of a *school turnaround*. Allow me, dear reader, to introduce myself—I am Neal Libertas, Esquire, a most distinguished gentleman of modern thought, and though my reputation precedes me, I assure you it is only partly earned. My methods, while vigorous, are entirely respectable, and my effects, though sometimes lamentable, are absolutely necessary for the improvement of our beloved academic institutions.

I confess, my humble origins were in boardrooms rather than ballrooms, but I was never one for idle flirtations. My heart has always been betrothed to the pursuit of "efficiency" and "reform." From the moment I set foot in the halls of education, I knew it was my duty to reshape it—to transform these quaint institutions of learning into paragons of *market-driven* excellence.

Upon my first arrival at Longbourn College, I was met with suspicion— "Who is this Mr. Libertas, and why does he demand we measure our success with such precision?" the gentlefolk murmured. But soon, I endeared myself to the faculty. I offered them incentives, you see—grand, sweeping proposals of "merit pay" and "performance-based funding." They could not resist. And though it was a scandalous match, the union of neoliberalism and academia was, at last, consummated.

Ah, but it was not without sacrifice, dear reader. The most delicate institutions—those underperforming schools of lesser fortune—were left to wither under my watch. I tried, truly I did, to extend my hand to them, but alas, they were *never* suited for the grand ball of success. I swept away their professors with the lightest touch, assured them they were simply not suited for this elegant dance card of modern education.

Now, I am often found promenading through the finest universities, whispering sweet nothings of accountability. My greatest pleasure? When I hear the polite applause of trustees at the news of a new fiscal victory, despite the absence of students in the lecture halls.

I am, above all things, a gentleman. And though my ways may seem severe, I assure you, I only seek to elevate. After all, who would question the manners of a man whose very name conjures images of "freedom"? So I leave you with this: the cost of progress, though steep, is but a small price to pay for the future I promise—a future as polite and calculating as the finest ballroom.

End Transmission by the Lorekeeper. "It is a truth universally acknowledged that Mr. Libertas is insufferable."

Neal Libertas: An Autobiography

Kawaii Sanrio Edition
By: The Players
Logged by the Lorekeeper

Konnichiwa, mina-san! I'm NeLi-chan, the cutest little harbinger of market-based education reform you ever did see! Don't let my big eyes and tiny fangs fool you—I'm here to make sure schools run just like businesses, with lots of cute data and *efficiency* stickers! NeLi-chan loves numbers, graphs, and making sure only the *best* schools get the shiny rewards. \(≧∪≦)/

Once upon a time, schools were all about teaching and learning—but NeLi-chan knew something was missing. How could schools be kawaii and *competitive*? So I scurried through the halls of education, spreading my philosophy of "choice"—where only the strongest schools thrive, and the weak ... well, NeLi-chan may look small, but I have a biiig appetite for *underperforming* institutions. (*∩ω∩*)

Here's what NeLi-chan loves to see:

- Schools competing for resources, like a magical scavenger hunt! Only, instead of treasure, it's funding! (o´∀`o)
- Teachers working hard for merit badges! No slacking, or NeLi-chan will nom-nom-nom your funding. (*^‿^*)
- Students treated like adorable little customers who need to get the best deal on their future! Only the top schools get the sparkly credits, though. (*ˆ3ˆ)

But NeLi-chan knows not everyone can be a star. Sometimes, I have to say goodbye to the schools that can't keep up. I give them a cute little wave and a sad emoji sticker as they fade away. (˙•ω•˙) Bye-bye, small school! NeLi-chan will miss you! ♡But only a little. 🌟 (｡♥‿♥｡)

End Transmission by the Lorekeeper. "Don't be fooled by NeLi-chan's sparkly exterior and heart-shaped emojis—underneath all that kawaii, she's like Hello Kitty with a debt collector's soul. But hey, at least she waves goodbye with a smile. (●‿●✿)/"

Neal Libertas: An Autobiography

Shakespearean Tragedy Edition
By: The Players
Logged by the Lorekeeper

(Enter Neal Libertas, cloaked in shadows, speaking in soliloquy.)

Oh, most foul and treacherous fortune!
Brought forth from the privatization's womb,
Was I, Neal Libertas, born of neoliberal doom,
To feast upon the ruin of knowledge's temple,
To set ablaze the hallowed halls of learning.
No kingdom's crown do I desire, nor riches grand,
But the sweet taste of profit, and lands unmanned.

Act I: The Fall of Academia
In times past, the schools stood proud,
Fost'ring minds in nurturing's name.
But I, with serpent's tongue, did whisper:
"Compete, or perish, 'tis nature's way,
For knowledge is no gift—'tis but a coin to trade."
The wise did falter, the noble schools did sway,
Their coffers emptied, students led astray.

Act II: The Betrayal
Thou call'st me tyrant? Aye, 'tis true,
I promised merit, yet gave chains.
For what is learning, if not measured by the weight
Of gold, of scores, of metrics plain?
Under mine watch, the weakest fell first,
And none did weep, for they knew the cost.
Thus did I, Neal, eat the underperforming,
Sate my hunger upon the bones of failure.
Fair Verona wept, for her schools were naught,
But I, untouched, did prosper and grow.

Act III: The Soliloquy of Neal Libertas
Why doth the world call me cruel,
When I but play the game they laid?
Is not the fairest man who doth compete
And win, whilst others fade?
Hark! The noble scholars call me beast,
Yet 'tis they who fall, prey to their own feast.

Alas! I sought but freedom, in trade and market fair.
But now, 'tis solitude that fills mine lair.
I am no man, no god—nay, I am a thing,
Of neoliberal birth, a monstrous king.
A prince of metrics, crowned by empty chairs,
No students left to cry of their despairs.

Act IV: The Fall of Neal
Yet shadows creep upon my soul,
For though I won, I paid a toll.
Empty are the halls I did control,
For all the world, now vacant, leaves me whole
In bitter ruin. What profit is there left to claim,
When none are left to speak my name?

(Curtain falls.)

End Transmission by the Lorekeeper. "And so doth Neal Libertas, king of nothing, fall."

Challenge from the Lorekeeper

"Brave readers, the tale of Neal Libertas has been retold many times, and yet ... I suspect there are more versions lurking in the shadowy recesses of your imagination. Now, it is your turn. I challenge you to create your own absurd edition of Neal's story, catering to an entirely new audience. Here are some premises to get your creative juices flowing:"

Scottish Accent Edition: "Ach, laddie! Picture Neal Libertas in the rugged Highlands, chomping down on schools like they're haggis. His downfall? When the clans rise up, armed with nothing but kilts and the spirit of freedom!"

Bridgerton Aura: "Dear Reader, it has come to this author's attention that Mr. Libertas has, yet again, left scandal in his wake. While his reforms may seem quite dashing, do not be fooled—his true aim is not the betterment of education, but the advancement of his own rank. Oh, the drama!"

Smut Manhwa: "Neal Libertas, the brooding CEO of Neoliberal Inc., finds himself irresistibly drawn to the underperforming universities he's meant to destroy. Will he crush them beneath the weight of economic reform—or will love (and scandalous plot twists) prevail in the boardroom?"

Alien Invasion Version: "Neal Libertas's appetite for education reform is, in fact, a cosmic hunger—his true form a giant, tentacled alien, sent to devour underperforming planets ..."

End Transmission by the Lorekeeper. "Now go forth, readers, and may your retellings of Neal Libertas be as absurd as they are unparalleled in creativity."

* * *

Challenge Three: Critical Romance Theory (CRT)

She stood at the edge, the cold wind biting,
Water below, the sky above—
"You jump, I jump," he whispered,
A vow made in a world that could not bear their love.
No lifeboats for this kind of devotion,
No place in history's safe harbor.
Yet still they leapt, heart to heart,
Into a future that none could see,
Save for the love that bound them,
In defiance of all that would pull them apart.

Lorekeeper's Premise

"In this world, the tragic story of the *Titanic* is anything but a romance—it's a crime. 'You jump, I jump,' a promise that transcends law and fate, now illegal. Heterosexual love has been outlawed, and whoever reads these forbidden words is swiftly fired, their books and legacies tossed overboard like lifeboats that never launched. The poem? Censored. The history? Erased."

Now, your task is simple: defend the importance of preserving CRT. For if you fail, the very essence of love—any love—will sink into the cold abyss, never to resurface.

The Lorekeeper pauses, glancing at each of *you* in turn. "Now, before I lay down the possible strategies, I must remind you: *think of your own approaches first*. We wouldn't want to influence your creativity too much—our job here is mostly to stir the ... pot. So, don't rely on us for a serious solution. But if you must, here's what we've come up with so far ..."

Defending CRT: Stirring the Pot Edition

- Bake Sale for Love:
  Host a bake sale to raise awareness for *Critical Romance Theory*. Themed treats (Mr. Darcy's Scones, Juliet's Croissants) come with pamphlets on the importance of romance in education.

- Secret Underground Romance Book Club:
  Form a secret book club to read banned romance novels, using innocent-sounding titles as cover. Meetings are held in obscure locations, like janitor closets or under bleachers.

  For example:

  ♥ Original: *Pride and Prejudice* by Jane Austen
  New Title: **Teatime and Casual Judgments**
  (A delightful story about sipping tea while mildly disapproving of people. No whirlwind romances or arrogant men reforming here.)

  ♥ Original: *Wuthering Heights* by Emily Brontë
  New Title: **How to Make Friends in the Wind**
  (Two people hang out on a windy hill ... definitely not filled with unhinged obsession or emotional manipulation. Just windy, friendly times.)

- ♥ Original: *Romeo and Juliet* by William Shakespeare
  New Title: **Two Teens Disobey Their Parents and Learn a Lesson**
  (A couple of rebellious teens ignoring parental advice. Certainly, no tragic romance or misunderstandings.)

- ♥ Original: *The Great Gatsby* by F. Scott Fitzgerald
  New Title: **Sparkly Parties and Totally Chill Friendships**
  (Just some friends throwing extravagant parties with zero existential crises or unrequited love. Very relaxed, no big deal.)

- ♥ Original: *Jane Eyre* by Charlotte Brontë
  New Title: **How to Get a Job and Mind Your Business**
  (A well-behaved governess goes about her duties without any distractions from brooding employers or mysterious wives. Totally professional.)

- ♥ Original: *Anna Karenina* by Leo Tolstoy
  New Title: **Train Etiquette and Very Happy Marriages**
  (A polite guide to catching trains and having entirely fulfilling and uncomplicated relationships. Nothing dramatic, no trains involved at all, really.)

- ♥ Original: *The Notebook* by Nicholas Sparks
  New Title: **A Diary of Birdwatching Adventures**
  (A wholesome look at the joys of writing daily notes—especially about birds. Definitely no heartbreak or epic romance that spans decades.)

- ♥ Original: *Gone with the Wind* by Margaret Mitchell
  New Title: **A Guide to Southern Gardening**
  (Just some tips on growing flowers and keeping your plantation … in the nicest, most genteel way possible. Love and war? Nah, just rosebushes.)

- ♥ Original: *A Room with a View* by E. M. Forster
  New Title: **Travel Tips: Finding the Best Windows**
  (It's all about appreciating architectural views and nothing else. Definitely not about forbidden romance on vacation.)

- ♥ Original: *Dr. Zhivago* by Boris Pasternak
  New Title: ***Snowball Fights and Other Winter Fun***
  (An adventurous romp in the snow! No civil wars, no tragic love triangles. Just snowmen and hot cocoa.)

- Dramatic Flash Mob:
  Stage a public re-enactment of iconic romantic scenes from banned books, complete with impassioned recitations. The authorities will either shut it down or be so charmed they join in.

- Unburnable Love Letter Chain:
  Distribute unburnable love letters on fireproof paper, spreading the message of CRT. If confiscated, the letters become indestructible proof of love's resilience.

- Blank Protest Signs:
  Protest for CRT with completely blank signs. They represent "the silenced love" and provoke a stand-off with authorities who demand words, only to find there's nothing to censor.

The Lorekeeper grins. "And there you have it—a fine collection of strategies to defend love in the most absurd way possible. But remember, dear players, the real question is: how far will you go to preserve *Critical Romance Theory*?"

* * *

Challenge Four: The Dung Beetle Dilemma: Academia at Ground Level

Lorekeeper's Premise

"You've faced many trials, but none so absurd as this. Prepare yourselves, for in this round, you will be transformed—into dung beetles."

The Lorekeeper waves a hand, and suddenly you feel yourself shrinking ... shrinking ... until your world tilts at an odd angle, and your new dung beetle legs twitch to life.

"As beetles, you must now roll your own ball of academic discourse, just as you've seen before. But to escape this adorable transformation, there is only one solution: observe the academic world from your beetle's perspective and find one element that you believe summarizes the essence of academia. Only then can you break the spell."

Instructions

Transformation: you are now dung beetles, stuck at ground level, forced to view academia through the lens of the absurd.

The Task: To break the spell, you must name or find *one* element that they think encapsulates their understanding of academia. It can be anything—an object, a concept, even a particular experience that reveals what academia means to you.

Lorekeeper's Open Ending

"And so, dear players, you find yourselves at a crossroads. What will you choose as your defining element of academia? The theories rolled endlessly through seminars? The jargon you've carried, polished, and reshaped? Or something else entirely?

The spell can only be broken by a single word that speaks to your truth. I invite you now, beetles and readers alike, to contemplate: what is *your* word that captures the essence of academia?"

Player Four

The Ultimate X Collab™
Bromance, the Fan Page, and the Zen Vibe

She walks in beauty,
But not enough syllables,
To say what I mean.

Analogies are often used in teaching as a shortcut to explain complex concepts by linking them to more familiar ideas. While this approach can provide students with an entry point to new material, it often ends up reinforcing the centrality of the culture from which the analogy is drawn. Rather than fostering genuine understanding, these analogies tend to solidify existing biases and misconceptions. As educators, when we draw simplistic parallels—like equating *Liang Shanbo and Zhu Yingtai*[5] to

---

5 *Liang Shanbo and Zhu Yingtai*, often referred to as the *Butterfly Lovers*, is a famous Chinese legend of two star-crossed lovers. Zhu Yingtai, disguised as a boy to attend school, meets Liang Shanbo, and the two develop a deep bond. However, Liang remains unaware of Zhu's true identity. By the time he discovers that Zhu is a woman, she has been promised to another man by her family. Heartbroken, Liang dies of grief. On the day of Zhu's wedding, she visits Liang's grave, and in an act of ultimate love, the grave opens, and Zhu jumps in. The two lovers are transformed into butterflies, flying away together, symbolizing their eternal love. The tale, often likened to *Romeo and Juliet* due to its themes of tragic love, has been adapted into various forms of art, including opera, ballet, and film, and remains one of China's most enduring love stories.

Romeo and Juliet, or *The Analects* to *The Republic*—we are guilty of a behavior that tethers learning to a single cultural narrative, often Western, that is seen as the "norm." This practice reinforces a centrality that marginalizes other perspectives, making students view non-Western texts and ideas as mere "versions" of familiar Western concepts. In reality, these analogies reduce the richness and nuance of different cultural discourses into easily digestible, and often stereotypical, sound bites.

According to Said's (1978) Orientalism, such educational shortcuts risk perpetuating the Western gaze, where Eastern cultures are viewed through a simplified, exoticized lens. When teachers rely on such analogies, they inadvertently deepen students' misconceptions, creating a veneer of understanding without genuine intellectual engagement. Giroux (2011) similarly critiques how this oversimplified pedagogy mirrors the neoliberal push for fast, efficient learning outcomes, where complexity is sacrificed for clarity and depth is exchanged for speed. By presenting these easy analogies, students are fed the illusion of understanding, but they remain bounded by the ideologies of their own culture, particularly when this culture is dominant within academic institutions. Furthermore, Spivak's (1999) concept of epistemic violence becomes relevant here, as the reliance on Western-centric analogies in classrooms silences *the Other*, reducing Eastern philosophies, stories, and intellectual traditions to mere reflections or distortions of Western ones. This process not only limits the students' capacity for deep learning but also reinforces hegemonic structures of knowledge production.

Posthumanism and Postqualitative Centrality

The reliance on Western-centric analogies in teaching is an arrogant educational "shortcut"—it reflects a broader ontological issue of centering certain modes of knowledge while marginalizing others. From a posthumanist perspective, this centrality mirrors the very anthropocentric frameworks that posthumanism seeks to dismantle. However, in educational spaces dominated by Western analogies, this relational thinking becomes constrained by a *cultural centrism* that privileges certain bodies of knowledge over others. The analogies that reduce

Eastern narratives to mere mirrors of Western classics reinforce a hierarchy where one culture, often the West, is seen as the epistemological center. Such approach not only negates the *decentralizing* project of posthumanism but also perpetuates a coloniality of knowledge, where other ways of knowing are subsumed under the dominant framework. As Mignolo (2011) writes, the "coloniality of power" extends to how knowledge itself is produced and disseminated, with Western narratives positioned as universal while others are rendered particular.

In postqualitative inquiry, this issue is even more pressing. Postqualitative thinking seeks to break away from the rigid structures of predefined categories, binaries, and grand narratives. It challenges the humanist tradition of fixed meaning and seeks to embrace fluid, emergent processes of understanding (St. Pierre, 2013). When analogies are used to create false equivalences between culturally distinct concepts, they *tether* students—and teachers—to a rigid, linear form of knowledge production that runs counter to postqualitative methods. The analogy itself becomes a form of epistemic closure, preventing the more rhizomatic (Deleuze & Guattari, 1987) exploration of meaning that postqualitative inquiry aims for. Moreover, the Western-centric analogy is a form of control—a way to *contain* difference within a framework that is intelligible to the dominant culture. In doing so, it resists the posthumanist goal of embracing multiplicity and difference. By anchoring everything to Western thought, these analogies reduce the possibility for "transversal learning"—learning that cuts across cultural, philosophical, and material boundaries, as Braidotti (2013) envisions.

In conclusion, this centrality of Western thought in education simultaneously undermines the plurality that posthumanism and postqualitative inquiry seek to embrace as well as highlights the ongoing issue of epistemological dominance. The result is not a deepening of cross-cultural understanding but a further entrenchment of cultural stereotypes. As such, the question becomes not just about the efficacy of analogies in teaching but about how we can challenge and disrupt these cultural juxtapositions to foster genuine understanding. This brings us to the central research question of this round of the gameplay:

How do superficial cultural analogies in education reinforce stereotypes and obstruct deeper cultural understanding, particularly in the context of East-West academic discourse?

This inquiry aims to critically examine the pedagogical practice of using analogies, especially those rooted in Western hegemony, and their effects on learning outcomes, cultural perceptions, and intellectual diversity in academic spaces. Through this lens, we will explore how the players navigate these flawed analogies in the forthcoming game setting, engaging with and resisting the limitations of educational "shortcuts."

Game Setting: The Ultimate X Collab

Welcome to the ultimate fusion of cultural chaos, where sense and reason are left at the door, and wild analogies reign supreme. In this game, players are invited to create cultural "collaborations" by merging completely unrelated analogies and references. The Lorekeeper, ever watchful (and slightly satirical), will push them to find the most far-fetched and nonsensical combinations, all while chuckling at the inevitable loss of meaning in their analogies.

Challenges
1. **Folklore Mashup™:**
   The players are tasked with creating the most improbable "collab"—Folklore Mashup™ (a proudly ridiculous trademark)—by merging classical Asian folklore with Greek myth, Disney stories, Brothers Grimm fairy tales, and more. Imagine the *Monkey King* and *Hercules* teaming up to retrieve Cinderella's lost glass slipper from Hades, or *Snow White* throwing down with Mulan over who reigns supreme in the underworld. The possibilities? Absolutely nonsensical.

2. **K-Pop Reigns™:**
   Players must form a K-Pop band using characters from global folklore, mythology, and culture. The challenge is to blend

K-Pop's flashy, polished aesthetic with wildly out-of-place cultural icons. Will Confucius learn to moonwalk, or will Socrates finally drop the hottest verse of the century? Can Aphrodite and Athena put their rivalry aside to become the ultimate duo? Prepare for a cross-cultural debut unlike anything seen before (and probably never to be repeated).

3. **Poetic Translation Fail™:**
Players will attempt to translate between vastly different forms of poetry—like squeezing *Haiku* into the grandiosity of Western Romanticism. The results will likely be *gloriously catastrophic*. Have you ever tried condensing *Byron* into three lines of 5-7-5? No? Well, you're about to. Words will break, meanings will crumble, and somewhere in the chaos, you might even catch a glimpse of literary brilliance—or at the very least, resigned chuckle.

"That sounds fun." One of the players piped up, a local student who was thoroughly steeped in Western culture.

"Would you like to dub yourself an avatar?" I asked, ever the diligent (and overly invested) Lorekeeper.

"Michelle," she said with a grin.

Of course. Michelle. Not just any *Michelle*, but surely the shadow of Michelle Yeoh loomed large behind this choice. This so-called local student, who appeared to be a staunch defender of Western culture, secretly harbored a love for *Wuxia*—specifically, for a certain film that I had never seen, but whose title was whispered with reverence: *Crouching Tiger, Hidden Dragon*. I had a sneaking suspicion that Michelle, the avatar, was about to deliver something beyond cultural juxtapositions.

On a different note, I suddenly recalled a rather amusing incident that cemented Michelle's identity as an off-brand Wuxia heroine.

Michelle, despite her love for gardening, had one small problem—she was mildly allergic to sunlight. Naturally, this created a bit of a paradox for someone who enjoyed working outdoors. Always one to lean into the absurd, I once brought her back a gift from a quick trip to Asia: a tea-picking umbrella. You know, one of those ethereal canopies farmers wear while working in the fields, providing shade like a floating crown above their heads. The moment I gave it to her, she was smitten. she donned it immediately, as though she had stepped straight out of a *Wuxia* epic. The umbrella completed her transformation into a low-budget Michelle Yeoh, but, as with all things too good to be true, there was a slight problem:

The tea-picking umbrella, while beautifully atmospheric, wasn't as practical as I had imagined. It tended to block her vision at inopportune moments, and more than once I watched in mild horror as she unwittingly bumped into obstacles while wandering about her garden, like some sort of graceful yet directionally challenged martial artist. And yet, despite the bumps and near-miss collisions with low-hanging branches, she insisted on wearing it every time she was out, convinced it gave her the gravitas of a *Wuxia* warrior in retirement, cultivating plants rather than defeating enemies. The visual of her, sweeping through her garden with this majestic yet mildly impractical umbrella, remains etched in my mind. Michelle might not have been an international action star, but she certainly lived the role, obstacles and all.

"You in? Any avatar in mind?" I asked, turning to the other player, an international student from East Asia who had been a key ally when I first started thinking about establishing a Center for Intercultural Studies on campus. Even after her graduation, we kept in touch, her insightful suggestions always adding depth to our ongoing conversations.

"... Astra," she said, somewhat sheepishly.

Of course. Astra.

This one, despite her deep cultural roots, was secretly a massive fan of Riot Games. *Valorant* was her stage, and her favorite character? Astra, the cosmic controller, one of the hardest roles to master in the tactical shooter.

For those unfamiliar with *Valorant*, it's one of Riot Games' most successful titles, a tactical first-person shooter (FPS) where players take on roles called "agents"—each with unique abilities. Astra, hailing from Ghana, is a "controller" agent, which means she excels at managing the battlefield by controlling key areas with smokes, stuns, and gravity wells. Her cosmic abilities allow her to manipulate the map from a higher, strategic plane, placing stars on the battlefield that she can later activate to block vision, pull enemies in, or concuss them. She requires precision, planning, and deep game sense—qualities not everyone can master, but this player could.

Now, here's the thing. People often say things like, "Wow, girls can be good gamers on varsity teams?" as though that's somehow surprising. But the truth is, it's as nonsensical as being surprised that girls can solve complex math problems or excel in rocket science. This player was, without a doubt, one of the best controllers I'd seen, making critical plays that turned the tide of games. It wasn't because she was defying some gendered expectation—it was because she was simply a brilliant gamer, full stop.

* * *

Challenge One: Folklore Mashup™:

Index Cards

East Pile

1. **Abe no Seimei**
   A legendary onmyoji (sorcerer) who dealt with spirits and demons in ancient Japan. Known for his wisdom and powers of divination, Seimei protected the capital from malevolent spirits.
   - Vibe: A mysterious figure navigating between the realms of the living and the dead, balancing forces of nature and fate.

2. **Kumiho** (Nine-Tailed Fox)
   In Korean folklore, the Kumiho is a fox spirit that can transform into a beautiful woman. Often portrayed as deceptive, she seeks to eat human hearts but may also seek redemption.
   - Vibe: Seductive yet tragic, trapped between human desires and spiritual redemption.

3. **Momo Taro**
   A hero from Japanese folklore, Momo Taro (Peach Boy) was born from a giant peach and raised by an elderly couple. He embarks on a journey to defeat ogres with the help of animal companions.
   – Vibe: A classic heroic tale with a strong connection to nature and loyalty.

4. **Princess Kaguya**
   A moon princess who was found as a baby in a bamboo stalk. She grows into a beautiful woman with many suitors but ultimately returns to the moon, revealing her celestial origins.
   – Vibe: Ethereal beauty and a sense of longing for another world, where earthly connections are fleeting.

5. **The Cowherd and the Weaver Girl**
   A tragic love story in Chinese mythology about two lovers separated by the Milky Way. They can only meet once a year when a bridge of magpies forms across the stars.
   – Vibe: Celestial romance, star-crossed lovers fated to be apart, with a bittersweet connection to the cosmos.

6. **Bai Suzhen** (The Legend of the White Snake)
   A mythical Chinese figure, Bai Suzhen is a white snake spirit who falls in love with a human. Their love story is fraught with obstacles, as Bai Suzhen faces persecution from a Buddhist monk.
   – Vibe: A tragic romance between a human and a spirit, rich with themes of transformation, loyalty, and the tragic consequences of love across different realms.

West Pile

1. **Hades and Persephone**
   The Greek myth of the god of the underworld abducting Persephone, who becomes his queen. Their love is tied to the cycle of seasons.
   – Vibe: A dark, seductive romance that plays with themes of death and rebirth, as well as the balance between life and death.

2. **The Little Mermaid**
   Hans Christian Andersen's tale of a mermaid who gives up her voice for love, only to face the tragic consequences of her choice.
   - Vibe: Tragic beauty, the sacrifice of identity, and an unfulfilled longing for love.

3. **Medusa**
   In Greek mythology, Medusa was a beautiful maiden cursed by Athena, turning her into a monster whose gaze could turn men to stone. She is often viewed as a symbol of victimhood and female rage.
   - Vibe: A tragic figure of beauty transformed into terror, representing themes of transformation, victimhood, and isolation.

4. **Prometheus**
   In Greek mythology, Prometheus stole fire from the gods to give to humanity, suffering eternal punishment for his defiance. He is often seen as a symbol of rebellion and the pursuit of knowledge.
   - Vibe: The visionary who suffers for his wisdom, with themes of sacrifice and the struggle for progress.

5. **Sigurd (Siegfried)**
   A hero from Norse mythology (also found in Germanic legend), Sigurd famously slays the dragon Fafnir. He is celebrated for his courage and cunning but ultimately ensnared in tragic love and betrayal.
   - Vibe: Heroism tainted by tragedy, where victory leads to deeper emotional and moral consequences.

6. **Rumpelstiltskin** (Brothers Grimm)
   The cunning dwarf who can spin straw into gold but demands a high price—ultimately trying to take the miller's daughter's firstborn child unless she can guess his name.
   - Vibe: A dark, mysterious figure whose power lies in secrecy and manipulation, entwined with themes of greed and desperation.

At the Lorekeeper's prompt, Astra stepped forward, eyeing the deck of index cards as though they might bite. She drew one: *Abe no Seimei*.

"Alright, folks," she began, awkwardly adjusting her stance as if she were about to drop some serious wisdom, "Abe no Seimei ... so, uh, he's like this legendary onmyoji—basically a sorcerer—who handled spirits and demons in ancient Japan. He was super OP, like a one-man supernatural police force or something. Basically, if you messed with the spirit world, this guy would show up, throw down some sick spells, and boom—problem solved."

The others blinked at her, trying to keep up.

"And ... that's all I got." Astra shrugged, clearly hoping she could leave it at that.

But no. The Lorekeeper was ever pushy. "Now, please provide an analogy, in Western terms," I said, my eyes gleaming with absurd challenge.

Astra's eyes darted, searching for inspiration. "It's like ... it's like ... uh ..." She struggled, the pressure building. "Okay, wait, I got it—he's kinda like *Doctor Strange*. You know? He's the protector of the mystical realms, super powerful, can banish demons, and sees through all the magical BS. Except Abe no Seimei did it with way less cape, and more ... calligraphy."

The Lorekeeper gave a long, slow blink, and with a completely straight face, muttered, "Yes, because clearly, calligraphy has never been more powerful to counter strike all those magical BS. Thank you, Astra, for your service to ancient Japanese mythology and pop culture." I motioned to Michelle. "Now, your turn to dazzle us."

With her ever-present air of quiet confidence, Michelle stepped up and drew her card. She glanced at it and gave a small, almost imperceptible smirk: *Prometheus*.

"So," she began, clearing her throat, "Prometheus was this rebellious titan who stole fire from the gods and gave it to humans. For this grand act of defiance, Zeus had him chained to a rock, where an eagle would come by every day and, um ... snack on his liver. But since he was immortal, his liver grew back every night, and the eagle would return to repeat the whole thing. This went on for, you know, an eternity or so."

The others nodded, visibly impressed by her surprisingly coherent retelling. Michelle wasn't done. "And, you know, Prometheus did this because he believed humans deserved fire, even if it meant eternal punishment. Classic self-sacrificing hero—big *I'm-right-even-when-I'm-wrong* energy."

She paused dramatically before delivering the kicker. "He's like … *Guo Jing*, from *The Legend of the Condor Heroes*. You know, loyal to a fault, always putting others before himself, and willing to endure endless suffering for the sake of the greater good. Only, you know, with Prometheus, the suffering involves an eagle and a liver, while Guo Jing's suffering is … mostly emotional trauma. Same heroism though, different bird."

For those of you who didn't grow up binge-reading Wuxia novels, let me introduce *Guo Jing*, the hero created by the legendary author, *Jin Yong*. Known for his unwavering loyalty, straightforwardness, and often being a bit too noble for his own good, Guo Jing is the quintessential hero. Raised by Mongols, trained in martial arts, and always tangled up in matters of honor and duty, he's the kind of guy who'd probably throw himself into eternal liver-regeneration if it meant saving humanity.

"And yes, there's an actual bird in his story, so thank you, Michelle, for keeping that theme alive." Says the Lorekeeper.

"Now," I continued, "we have all the players on the board. Abe no Seimei, the mystical sorcerer with impeccable calligraphy; Prometheus, the titan of fire, liver, and bird-related punishment; and of course, Guo Jing—our bird-whispering, morally indestructible hero … plus a Dr. Strange from nowhere. Time to weave these legends together into the Ultimate X Collab™ story of absurdity and wonder."

Folklore Mashup™: *A Saga of Sorcery and Sacrifice*

In an ancient forest, Abe no Seimei—mystic, onmyoji, and occasional practitioner of calligraphy with suspicious vibes—stood at the edge of a dimensional rift. Next to him (hovering just above the ground) was none other than Dr. Stephen Strange, his cape swirling dramatically in a wind (that seemed to follow him everywhere.)

The rift crackled with power, threatening to tear open a portal to worlds unknown. Seimei frowned, his brush tapping against his chin. "This is no ordinary breach in space-time," he murmured, "but the work of ... birds."

Dr. Strange raised an eyebrow. "You mean—like, metaphorical birds, right? Or are we talking literal?"

"No," Seimei intoned solemnly, "literal. And they're after livers. I've seen this before."

Just as Strange opened his mouth to question the absurdity of the situation, a screech echoed through the air. The sky darkened, and descending upon them came an enormous eagle—its eyes glowing, its wings spanning the heavens.

"Ah," Seimei remarked, a touch of satisfaction in his voice, "there it is. Prometheus' bird. I thought we'd run into this problem."

Meanwhile, in a forgotten corner of the underworld, Prometheus, his liver constantly regenerating only to be devoured, cast his weary eyes toward the horizon. But this time, instead of facing his usual torment alone, a lone figure approached: Guo Jing, hero of the Mongols, famed martial artist, and protector of the people.

Prometheus, his chains rattling softly, gave a weak laugh. "I thought I was the only one fated for endless suffering," he rasped.

Guo Jing, bowing respectfully, replied, "The world is full of suffering, Prometheus. But you don't have to carry this burden alone." He reached up, effortlessly snapping the chains that had bound the titan for millennia, freeing him with the strength that came from his unwavering sense of honor.

And yet, in the distance, the sky darkened. Another eagle approached—perhaps Prometheus' old tormentor, or perhaps a new kind of trial altogether. As the two figures stood together, ready to face this next chapter of their intertwined fates, Prometheus gripped his side.

Guo Jing merely smiled. *"Even if you fall, I'll be here."*

(Back in the forest.)

Seimei and Strange had been exchanging incantations, their magic swirling in tandem as they prepared to face the incoming eagle. "Let's make this quick," Strange said, "I've got to get back to the Sanctum. My cloak's getting impatient."

Seimei smirked, inscribing a protective charm in the air, the characters glowing with an ethereal light. "Just another day saving the balance between worlds, Strange."

Together, their magic intertwined—Seimei's ancient sorcery and Strange's cosmic arts—and the rift began to close. Above them, the eagle screeched one last time before vanishing into the ether, leaving only a ripple behind.

In the underworld, Prometheus and Guo Jing stood victorious as well, the eagles driven back, the chains of torment shattered. Prometheus turned to Guo Jing, his heart heavy with emotions, "I've been bound for so long. I don't know how to live without suffering."

Guo Jing gave a quiet nod, staring into the endless horizon. *"Then let's find out together."*

(The End. For Now.)

* * *

Challenge Two: K-Pop Reigns™

Setting
Players will take turns using a random number generator to determine the fate of their soon-to-be catastrophic K-Pop group, *New StrataPlay*. The process unfolds in three absurdly entertaining steps:

Step 1: Genre Selection
Roll the generator to decide whether they'll form a girl band or a boy band:

1 = Girl band, 2 = Boy band
(The players roll a 1. It's a girl band.)

Step 2: Band Size
- Next, the players determine the number of members by rolling an integer from 2 to 6.
  (The players roll a 5—so they'll be forming a five-member girl band.)

Step 3: Member Selection
For each band member, the players will roll again to select the category from which the idol will be chosen:

- 1 = Classic or modern novels (East or West)
- 2 = Figures from traditional myth/folklore or modern-day anime (East or West)
- 3 = Deities (East or West)

The players must name their nominee based on the category rolled, diving into the absurd crossovers between cultural icons. Both players must agree on the nomination to successfully debut each member.

Final Outcome
Once all five members have been selected, the *New StrataPlay* group will be assembled in full. The final lineup of literary, mythological, and divine figures will be poised for their debut, blending K-Pop's glittering chaos with millennia of cultural significance (or irrelevance, depending on your perspective).

Let the audience witness the most original girl group to ever grace a K-Pop stage.

Fan Page: Introducing New StrataPlay—The K-Pop Group No One Saw Coming

Welcome, StrataFans! Prepare yourselves for the most mind-boggling debut in K-Pop history. Meet the members of *New StrataPlay*, a five-member global sensation blending ancient myth, classical literature, and divine intervention into one chaotic, glittering girl group.

Elizabeth Bennet (Lead Dancer)

- ♥ Origin: Pride and Prejudice (Jane Austen)
- ♥ Position: Lead Dancer, Sub-Vocalist
- ♥ Signature Move: The "Polite Pirouette"—because she'd never dare step out of line, even on stage.
- ♥ Personal Info: When not dancing, Elizabeth enjoys long walks through the moors and roasting suitors with witty commentary. She's also been known to exchange letters with her fellow band members in Austen-style prose, which no one has bothered to read yet. Allergic to insufferable men but is inexplicably okay with pride.

Athena (Main Rapper)

- ♥ Origin: Greek Mythology—Goddess of Wisdom and War
- ♥ Position: Main Rapper, Sub-Visual
- ♥ Signature Move: The "Battle Cry Drop"—a rap so fierce, it brings rival groups to their knees.
- ♥ Personal Info: In her spare time, Athena enjoys weaving complex battle strategies and offering wisdom to mortals (though most of her advice is wasted on them). She also collects olive trees and shields with *Aegis* designs, and has a not-so-secret love for epic poetry slams. Her ideal type? Anyone who can win a debate on ancient philosophy.

The Little Mermaid (Lead Vocalist)

- ♥ Origin: The Little Mermaid (Hans Christian Andersen)
- ♥ Position: Lead Vocalist, Sub-Dancer
- ♥ Signature Move: The "Tearful Trill"—her vocal runs are known to bring an audience to tears, mostly because they remind everyone of heartbreak.
- ♥ Personal Info: She spends her off-hours composing sad ballads about unrequited love and pining for sea foam. Her favorite snack is seaweed-flavored ice cream.

Guanyin (Visual, Center)

- ♥ Origin: Chinese Mythology—Goddess of Mercy
- ♥ Position: Visual, Center, Sub-Vocalist
- ♥ Signature Move: The "Serenity Spin"—a calming twirl that radiates peace and clears the mind of all worldly troubles.
- ♥ Personal Info: When she's not serving as the center of attention, Guanyin meditates, practices mindfulness, and occasionally listens to rain sounds on repeat. She also volunteers at kitten shelters and once single-handedly resolved a band argument with a smile. Her favorite color is *tranquil white*, and she's never been spotted in a bad mood. (She also has over a thousand hands but never brags about it.)

Joan of Arc (Main Dancer, Face of the Group)

- ♥ Origin: Historical/Mystical Figure
- ♥ Position: Main Dancer, Face of the Group
- ♥ Signature Move: The "Battlefield Boogie"—a dance routine so intense, it feels like she's leading her troops to victory with every step.
- ♥ Personal Info: Joan enjoys leading charge after charge, whether on the battlefield or the dance floor. She collects swords (mostly for the aesthetic), and her favorite movie is *Mulan*—though she insists she'd lead better. Her dream is to debut at the Notre-Dame Cathedral. Her motto: "Fight first, apologize never."

* * *

Challenge Three: Poetic Translation Fail™

Procedure

Players will take turns presenting a poem from their cultural roots—something meaningful, something grand, or perhaps something deceptively simple. They'll attempt to explain the meaning behind the poem to the best of their knowledge, unraveling its essence, rhythm, and beauty.

(Then the chaos begins.)

The rest of the players will put on their "resort to analogy" hats and offer their reimaginings of the masterpiece within the context of their own cultural roots. Whether it's squeezing *Lord Byron* into a three-line *Haiku* or turning a delicate *Tanka* into a grandiose *Ode*, the results are guaranteed to be poetic catastrophe or catastrophic brilliance.

Disclaimer: The Lorekeeper strongly recommends that you do **not** present your *favorite* poem. We wouldn't want your all-time favorite masterpiece to be mangled beyond recognition, only for you to wander this world forever more without it.

Astra began, "Okay, so, this one's from this dude named *Wang Wei*. He was like ... a big deal back in the Tang dynasty in China. His poems are all, like, super Zen and deep—kinda like nature meets philosophy meets ... chill vibes. You know?"

She continued, "So this line is basically like, '*You walk until the water runs out, and then you just sit there and watch the clouds do their thing.*[6]' It's super peaceful. Kinda like when you've done all your homework and you're just staring at your screen, waiting for the next thing to happen. Except instead of scrolling TikTok, you're watching clouds, which ... I guess is more poetic or whatever."

---

6 This line is derived from Wang Wei's poem 《终南别业》, specifically the verse "行到水穷处,坐看云起时," which translates more formally as "Walking to where the water ends, I sit and watch the clouds rise." Wang Wei, a renowned poet of the Tang dynasty, was known for integrating Buddhist thought into his poetry, particularly the themes of stillness, nature, and spiritual insight. In this moment, the poem reflects a sense of serenity found in reaching the physical and metaphorical end of a journey, only to embrace the quiet simplicity of nature's cycles. For more, see translations of and discussions on Wang Wei's poetry in *Chinese literary studies* (Cai, 2013).

She squinted the Lorekeeper and the other player, "Anyway, it's all about how you reach the end of something, and instead of freaking out, you just ... vibe with it. 'Cause sometimes, you gotta stop moving to, like, actually see stuff.'"

Reimagining

A "Zen vibe" Reflection on "You walk until the water runs out, and then you just sit there and watch the clouds do their thing"
(Texas Zen Style)

Well, I moseyed on down till the creek ran dry,
Plopped myself down, no need to try.
Them clouds up yonder, just floatin' around,
Like they got all day, ain't makin' a sound.
Ain't no rushin', no need to hurry,
Life's a slow ride, no room to worry.
The water's done, but them clouds sure fly—
Guess that's life, partner, no need to ask why.

Michelle began, "Alright, I picked a piece from Wordsworth, *I Wandered Lonely as a Cloud*. You might've heard of him—he's the one who practically invented *long walks* as a poetic theme. Anyway, this poem is all about him ... well, wandering around like a lonely cloud, obviously. You know, just floating over the hills and valleys, minding his own business. Classic daydreaming Brits."

"Then he spots a bunch of daffodils—like a crowd of them—just chilling by a lake, waving in the breeze. And suddenly, he's like, 'Wow, this is amazing!' It's all very *picturesque*. Nature, solitude, peaceful vibes. I think the whole point is he's supposed to feel connected to something bigger than himself ... because of flowers."

"And when he feels sad later, he remembers those daffodils and feels better. So, yeah ... it's like finding a *nature-based happy place* on your walk."

(Drum roll, please.)

Reimagining

(5-7-5 Style)

Clouds be floating high,
Flowers stand there—just chilling,
Uh, I feel … okay?

Player Five

Überfrau Manifesto
The Wolf, the Shards, and Storytelling Stories

> **DISCLAIMER:** The following gameplay contains content that may not be suitable for all readers. Themes of visibility, vulnerability, and self-fragmentation are explored in dark, surreal, and emotionally charged ways. The Lorekeeper strongly recommend proceeding with caution. Use of the *StrataPlay Safeword System* is encouraged for emotional or mental breaks during intense moments. Reader discretion is advised.
>
> **SAFEWORD GUIDE:**
>
> CD (Cool Down): Pause the chapter, take a break.
> OT (Out of Taunt): If the content is pushing too far, call out the Lorekeeper—skip ahead, leave the scene.
> GG (Good Game): The chapter ends here for you. #GameOver
>
> **SPECIAL NOTE:**
> The manically dramatic personality you will encounter in this particular game setting—namely, the Lorekeeper's deranged

musings—is an intentional narrative device designed to theatrically unveil the tensions and absurdities of societal expectations.

Your author has not, in fact, lost her mind, nor is it recommended to conduct any research studies involving cannibalism, the devouring of institutions, or the dismemberment of colleagues. Such approaches, though perhaps metaphorically intriguing, are not part of the StrataPlay methodology. Proceed with caution—and a healthy sense of irony.

[Opening Monologue]

You enter Thoughtspire, though you can't say why. Nor can you say for how long.

But here you are—all eyes on you. The weight of it presses against your skin, familiar, thrilling ... suffocating. It's a warmth that makes you ache, doesn't it? To be seen... and to be hunted.

"I see you," whispers the Lorekeeper. Her presence slithers around you, both soothing and menacing. You feel her gaze, but it's not a mere glance—it pierces, it pulls. She inspects, she waits. You want to slip into the shadows, but the light drags you back, inch by inch. The Lorekeeper offers you choices, but they all feel like traps.

You long for the cloak of "invisibility," a refuge from the eyes that judge and consume. And yet, you want to be "witnessed." You crave that intoxicating gaze. Admired. Desired.

But it burns, doesn't it? The longer they watch, the hotter it becomes, until you start to shrink. The paradox gnaws at you—wanting to be seen, fearing what you must offer in return.

How much will they take before you've given too much? How much of yourself will remain once they've dissected every piece? And here's the rub: Are you just another reflection of their desires? Or are you the one in control—deciding how much to reveal, how much to hide?

Game Setting

You, Player V, are under the Lorekeeper's scrutiny. Her gaze clings to you, whether it's because of your allure or something darker. She's fascinated by you—an ardent admirer, a fervent student, eager to learn everything you have to offer. But that admiration has a darker edge. She loathes you from time to time, whether it's because of an offhand comment you made or the way you dismissed her feelings without realizing. But in truth, you'll never know what sparked it. (Maybe it's your outfit.)

She worships you, *yes*, but that doesn't stop her from leaving a cutting comment on your *Rate My Professor* page or dropping a dagger of criticism in your end-of-semester evaluations. It's all for your own good, mind you. Like any good fan, she's just watching out for you, helping guide your growth. She's invested in your journey, your potential. She knows what's best.

The Challenge

You're tasked with navigating this strange, oppressive world where visibility and vulnerability are intimately linked. The Lorekeeper plays along, but there's little escape from her penetrating gaze—or from the public eye. She grants you moments of power, moments where you feel seen and admired, only to pull the rug from beneath you and make you wonder why you ever craved the spotlight in the first place.

The Lorekeeper's Pull

She's both your *supporter* and your *captor*. She wants you to believe she's at your mercy, perfectly tamed, obedient, always at your call. But in truth, she's the one in control—the one with the power to corrupt you. She's watching, waiting for the moment you think you're in charge, only to dominate you, mold you into something more manageable, more malleable. She tests your limits, slowly, methodically, watching you fracture under the pressure she's carefully applied. Her gaze is a force you can't resist. It's full of admiration and curiosity, and also the weight of expectation. And it makes you both yearn for her attention and dread the consequences of it.

Her voice cuts through the dark:

> *"Do you feel it? That desire to be liked, to be perfect in the eyes of those who watch ... and the agony of knowing you never will be? They'll rip you apart eventually. They always do."*

[Press Any Key to Continue] *(You may also try performing the Animenz version of "Unravel" to impress the Lorekeeper. No pressure.)*

The Lorekeeper greets you with a slow smile as *Thoughtspire* unfurls further before you, its winding halls pulsing with an eerie glow.

> *"Ah, Player V ... how delightful that you're still here."*

(Her gaze is heavy as she extends her hand toward the pathways ahead, each one shimmering with cryptic energies.)

> *"You stand at the threshold of many trials, each crafted with care just for you. But where will you begin? I'll leave that up to you ... for now."*

(The pathways ahead beckon, each marked with signs that seem to shift in and out of focus. You must choose. But choose wisely, dear Player V ...)

Challenge 1: The Masquerade of Validation

(A soft, distant melody drifts through the air—a haunting, delicate tune that crawls into your bones. Masked faces appear in the mist, flickering in and out of existence, each one eager, each one expectant.)

> "Here," the Lorekeeper whispers, *"you will dance for them all, Player V. Every mask craves something different from you. But how far will you bend before you lose yourself entirely in the performance?"*

(Eyes swirl around you, the weight of their gazes tugging at your edges, and the masks spin faster, swirling through the dim light. Each mask demands something new. Each promise of validation comes at a small cost.)

Challenge 2: A Prey in Thoughtspire: Hunter x Hunter

(The halls grow darker, shadows thickening as a low growl rumbles through the corridors. Two paths stretch ahead.)

To the left, *Capybeara* (yes, she's a bear, obviously) beckons with her soft paw, a playful grin spread across her face. Her movements are slow, almost too calm for the danger she promises to protect you from.

To the right, *Little Red* glares at you from beneath her *black-and-white* hood, her eyes flashing with defiance. Her world is monochrome, a study in rebellion against the rules imposed on her.

> *"You must choose your hunter,"* the Lorekeeper murmurs, her voice dripping with amusement. *"They will protect you ... won't they? Or perhaps they will simply guide you deeper into peril. After all, the prey always has a choice in its predator ... no?"*

(A chill creeps through the air as both paths beckon with their own dangers. Who do you trust, Player V? Which hunter will be your guide through the labyrinth of Thoughtspire?)

Challenge 3: Shards of You

(The sound of shattering glass echoes through the chamber as the floor beneath you begins to crack. Mirrors rise from the ground, lining the walls around you—each one showing a different reflection. But the images are fractured, distorted, broken.)

> *"Ah yes,"* the Lorekeeper muses, *"the fragments of you. The Desired you, the Despised you, the Visible you, the Vulnerable you ... perfectly scattered."*

> She circles you slowly, her voice dark and deliberate. *"Let's see how many pieces you can gather before there's nothing left. Will you reconcile them? Or will you embrace the chaos of being torn apart? Maybe you'll even find comfort in the fragments, accepting that some pieces were never meant to be whole."*

(The mirrors shimmer, their fractured images glinting in the dim light, waiting for you to make a choice.)

> The Lorekeeper's smile lingers as she watches you. *"Well? The challenges await, Player V, make a choice. We both know it's not a choice that you ... must always choose."*

* * *

The Masquerade of Validation

The air grows thick with expectation as the Lorekeeper smirks at your hesitation.

"Ready to be adored, Player V? Oh, don't worry—you're in good hands. All you have to do is please *everyone*. Simple, right?" Her tone is sugary-sweet, but you know better.

[First Boss Battle Triggered: "Bashō-san," The Haiku Frog]

A faint *ribbit* echoes from the shadows, and out hops Bashō-san, the famed Haiku-spouting frog. Uncannily similar to the legendary poet Matsuo Bashō, his amphibious form is draped in an old haori, and his beady eyes glint with wisdom—or perhaps just mischief. His tiny frog legs step lightly, yet his presence is as commanding as a master at a tea ceremony.

He clears his throat, and with a grandiose croak, he delivers his request, in 5-7-5, apparently:

> *"Inspiration lost,*
> *A double flip will revive—*
> *Leap, and I will write."*

Bashō-san fixes his gaze on you, unblinking.

(Lorekeeper's Commentary)

"Ah, sensei! お久しぶりでございます。お元気でいらっしゃいますか?" The Lorekeeper bows deeply, her tone dripping with the highest form of respect. "You honor us, as always, with your presence. Ever the perfectionist."

She then turns to you, her voice taking on a teasing lilt. "But surely you don't mind twisting yourself into something a little unnatural, do you, Player V? I mean, it's only a *double flip*. And think—just imagine the masterpiece he'll write if you impress him."

(You have no idea how to perform a double flip. But the Lorekeeper's gaze lingers, sharp as a blade, and Bashō-san sits silently, waiting. You don't want to disappoint either of them … do you?)

[Second Boss Battle Triggered: The Bunny by the Washroom]

(Before you can even catch your breath, a blur of pink bounds into view—The Bunny by the Washroom, who twirls in a frenzy of pastel hues.)

"You! Paint everything *pink*!" she shrieks. "The walls, the floor, and your soul! Everything must be pink! No exceptions!" Her fluffy paws are already smudged with the shade of bubblegum nightmares.

(Lorekeeper's Commentary)

"Ah, yes. Our dear Bunny does love her vision, doesn't she? And pink is so ... flattering, don't you think? Oh, Player V, you'll look 'positively delightful' when you're done."

(You feel the brush in your hand. The Lorekeeper smiles, her eyes glinting as if this was all a game to her. Oh, wait ... it is.)

[Third Boss Battle Triggered: The Gatekeeper]

(Suddenly, a stack of papers taller than you appears, accompanied by the imposing figure of *The Gatekeeper*. They push their glasses up and sigh, exuding the aura of eternal bureaucratic drudgery.)

"Please," they say, "I need you to reformat these files. Print them, handwrite them, scan them, submit them digitally, and then repeat the process. Twice." Their voice is calm but unwavering—this is not a suggestion.

(Lorekeeper's Commentary)

"So reasonable, don't you think? Just a bit of paperwork. After all, Player V, you do aim to please us all, right? It would be such a shame if The Gatekeeper felt undervalued. And surely, you can see how important it is to meet their, ah, ever-evolving standards. Besides," she adds with a wink, "it's only your sanity at stake."

[Fourth Boss Battle Triggered: Tomie]

Finally, a soft voice cuts through the madness—sweet and slightly off-kilter. Tomie slinks out from the shadows, her delicate features framed by an innocent smile.

"Oh, Player V," she coos. "You must be starving by now. Why not devour the entire school? It's just a snack, after all. A light meal. I'll even help you … if you want." She giggles, her eyes gleaming with an endearing invitation.

(Lorekeeper's Commentary)

"Well, well, Tomie's got quite the appetite, doesn't she? But don't worry, Player V. It's not really cannibalism if it's the institution you're consuming. Just think of it as … a rite of passage. You wouldn't want to disappoint her now, would you?"

The Lorekeeper's grin stretches wide as Tomie moves closer, urging you to give in, to the sweet satisfaction of being favored by all. And then, something shifts—almost imperceptibly at first, but it's there, lurking behind her carefully constructed composure. A flicker. A crack in the mask. And just like that, you started to hear the Lorekeeper's unvoiced monologue:

Lorekeeper's Stream of Consciousness

They don't even know, do they? They look at me and they see *her*—the poised, musical, ever-present Lorekeeper. The one with the answers, the one who watches, *guides* them through their absurd little labyrinth. But really, *really*, I just want to watch them squirm. Watch them bend, break, and devour themselves from the inside out. It's delicious. Every choice they make? It's mine. Every step they take? It's under my gaze, under my thumb, my control. How easily they twist themselves into knots, and for what? "Validation"? A nod of approval? *Hah*—as if I even care. As if any of this is real.

But I need them to think it is. That's the trick. Keep them tethered, but just enough slack so they believe they're still in control. Oh, but that's where it gets fun. Because at any moment—any moment—I can yank the chain. Tighten it. And when they look up, when their eyes finally meet mine … what will they see? Oh, I *know* what they'll see. The same thing I see every time I glance in the mirror. That hunger. That twisted little spark that says, *"Conform to it. Give in. Stop thinking. The world is perfect just as it is. Don't bother bending it. Bend yourself instead. Break yourself if you must. And all problems shall be solved."*

God, I want them to see it, from my point of view, up here on the stage—under the obscured spotlight.

It's ironic, isn't it? Being so highly visible, standing in the center of everything, and yet, feeling swallowed by a strange kind of *endarkenness*. The stage looms, dwarfing even the grandest instruments, making everything seem disproportionately diminutive, including you. The spotlight burns, but it doesn't illuminate—not really. Instead, it creates a hyper-visibility that distorts rather than reveals. You're being watched, but you can't see them; you know they're there, those countless eyes lurking in the shadows. This is what panopticon (Foucault, 1977) feels like. You can't pinpoint who's watching, but you know you're never alone. Sometimes those eyes adore you, shining with admiration, waiting for every movement, every word. But other times? They wait for your misstep. They're there to pounce, to point out the smallest flaw, eager to see you falter. You're both drawn to and repelled by the audience's gaze.

Funny, isn't it? How the tighter the spotlight focuses, the more isolated you become.

And it's visibility; it's transformation. Every gaze, every expectation, twists you into something else. It's not about performing anymore; it's about survival. You, the scholar, the artist, the professor, the life's performer—every facet of you bends beneath the weight of their expectations. Sartre's "the look" (1993) encapsulates this moment: the gaze of others transforms the subject into an object, a figure molded by external perceptions rather than internal authenticity. Under that relentless light, your world narrows to a single, monochrome plane—a black-and-white keyboard where you play the notes by heart.

Sheet music as guidance? Irrelevant. You couldn't read it even if you wanted to. The light consumes everything. Breathing? It becomes a performance too. Sometimes you forget to breathe at all, caught in the intensity of it. Other times, you're gasping for air, as if your lungs have forgotten their purpose. You're simply performing an identity shaped by the gazes around you (Butler, 1990). And the loneliness and self doubt? Oh, it's perpetual. To remain whole in this performance is to navigate these gazes without being shattered by them, yet the more you're seen, the more you fragment into reflections of what they desire (Braidotti, 2013).

But here's the kicker: it's simultaneously addictive. Terrifyingly so. That spotlight, so blinding it feels like divinity itself, is as seductive as it is isolating. In that narrow moment, it's as if you believe—no, *hope*—that someone, somewhere, will glimpse something extraordinary in you, the one imprisoned on stage. The thrill is intoxicating. The *abject*, as Kristeva might suggest, lies in this paradoxical relationship between the need for validation and alienation, as I hover between subject and object, between that which is seen and that which is unassimilable, abjected (Kristeva, 1980). It's not that I fear the act of being seen; I fear what that gaze strips away from me, how it leaves me fragmented and objectified, a mere reflection of others' desires.

The absurdity of it all—those 12-cm stilettos ... instruments of torture, if you ask me. But you wear them, defying gravity as you glide on to the stage, ready to perform and to please. The paradox of being desired yet despised, of wanting to perform yet fearing the vulnerability that comes with it, speaks to what I'd like to unveil in the Überfrau Manifesto: the struggles to exist as both autonomous and objectified, both powerful and fragile.

* * *

A Prey in Thoughtspire: Hunter x Hunter

Route R: (Little Red)

You decided to go with Little Red. There's something about her—those breathtaking emerald eyes, flashing with defiance—that catches your attention.

Red starts off casually, her voice calm and detached. "I never liked red," she muses. "But The Wolf ... he said it suits my eyes. Said I should wear it more. Makes me stand out." She pulls at her iconic riding hood—it's reversible. One side black and white, the other a vivid crimson. She's wearing it inside out now, the monochrome side showing first when you saw her. Beneath it all, is she a ... gothic lolita? You chuckle at the thought.

But something nags at you. You begin to wonder if she's trapped, manipulated by this Wolf. Red's tone may be nonchalant, but your decolonialist instincts spark to life. You can't help but suggest, "You shouldn't have to wear what he says. Choose for yourself. Fight back against these patriarchal clichés."

Red listens, then slowly turns toward you, her emerald eyes gleaming with an intensity you didn't expect. Her voice drops into something that's neither light nor dark, but eerily neutral.

> *"I have a question for you, Player V. If there are three wolves out there, and we killed one ... how many wolves are left?"*

(Your Choices:)
A. **Two—Simple math, right?** (skip to Ending R-BE)
B. **None—We don't stop fighting until we know we're safe, once and for all.** (skip to Ending R-HE)
C. **I'm going to call World Animal Protection.** (skip to Ending R-RE)

The Endings

R-BE: Bad Ending: The Eternal Return

History repeats itself. You realize, far too late, that wolves never truly die. You may have thought you struck one down, but even in defeat, they return—stronger, more cunning, more relentless. Each victory you celebrated was nothing but a fleeting moment, a fragile illusion of progress. The wolves are always there, lurking at the edges of the labyrinth, waiting for you to tire. You feel the weight of this truth settle in—this was never a fight you could win. It was always a cycle, repeating over and over, as endless as the twists and turns of Thoughtspire itself.

You're in the center of Nietzsche's (2006, 1974) concept of *eternal recurrence*, the idea that life, with all its struggles and victories, loops back on itself in endless repetition. The wolves become symbolic of this cycle, embodying the futility of resisting without real structural change. Without deeper transformation, you remain a prisoner, reliving the same battles, again and again. In this grand game, even your fight for autonomy becomes a performance, rehearsed in the shadows of those who came before. The wolves return, not because you failed, but because the system itself ensures they always will.

> *You have chosen to walk down this path, Player V. The labyrinth closes in, and the wolves grow stronger with each step. Eternal recurrence loops around you, trapping you in the never-ending cycle.*

Question: Now that you've realized the wolves never die, what's your next move? How do you resist, or will you continue the fight in futility? What strategies will you adopt to break the cycle if it even can be broken?

[S/L: Return to Main Menu.]
R-HE: "Happy" Ending: "The World Upside Down"

Red smiles slyly. The wolves, it turns out, are not the hunters—they are now her prey. Enslaved under her control, they wear the very chains they once used. Red parades them through the labyrinth—broken, submissive, utterly defeated. Her power is absolute now. As you watch this strange procession, something feels off. The thrill of victory rings hollow, twisted in its triumph.

You finally realized, power isn't a fixed entity to be simply won or transferred—it morphs, shifts, and reshapes those who wield it. In Red's victory, she becomes the very predator she once fought. The lines between oppressor and oppressed blur, showing how absolute power corrupts (Foucault, 1977). What began as a fight for autonomy has mutated into domination. The wolves, once a symbol of fear, are now the subjects of Red's authority, but at what cost? Power isn't liberating—it circulates, transforming those it touches. In Red's ascent, she takes on the very characteristics of the predator she sought to escape, exposing the paradox of freedom: in wielding power, she's no freer than the wolves she controls.

> *Little Red has turned the tables. The wolves now serve under her command, and the world you once knew has been turned upside down.*

Question: You've managed to flip the script, but at what cost? Now that you're in control, how will you wield this power? Will you protect or oppress? What kind of leader will you become?

    [S/L: Return to Main Menu.]
    R-RE: Real Ending: "**Über-Rot**"

Red stops and stares at you, then, with deliberate precision, she removes her hood. She is neither woman nor man, but something beyond—a cyborg, a super-red, *Über-Rot*. She wasn't being oppressed by the Wolf—she was the Wolf all along. Her movements are fluid, effortless, transcending the boundaries of human and animal.

"Wolves, humans ... these labels mean nothing to me. What matters is what *you* choose to see in me. I'm "Little Red" and many more. I am everything."

In this moment, Red becomes the embodiment of fluidity and multiplicity—an identity that refuses to be pinned down. She exists in a space beyond binaries, beyond categories of predator and prey. You realize now that what you've encountered is no ordinary being but a manifestation of the posthuman, an entity that defies conventional boundaries and definitions. You are reminded of Haraway's (1985)—Red, or rather Über-Rot, is the perfect example of a posthuman cyborg, transcending categories and rejecting the limitations imposed by binaries. She's no longer confined. She is a fluid, autonomous force, embodying the multiplicity of identities that exist in the posthuman world.

Route C: Capybeara

You find yourself face to face with Capybeara, her soft, innocent features catching you off guard. Her wide eyes twinkle with an unexpected charm. You've never imagined a bear could be ... *this* cute.

Capybeara: "Hiya, Player V. It's good to meet you. My mom always told me never to wander the labyrinth alone. You know, the Lorekeeper's always lurking somewhere ... strange, isn't she?"

Lorekeeper: "I can hear you, Capy, even with partial hearing loss. Thank you very much."

Capybeara chuckles sheepishly, then continues, "My mom said if I ever had to choose between following a player or a manbear—ugh, they're the worst—I should probably go with the player. You players ... well, sure, you might get violent and kill, but if you do, at least no one will ask what I was wearing when it happened. You're more direct. Clear intentions. Unlike the manbear ... they're always bearsplaining, hiding something under that *harmless* fur."

Her words tug at your heartstrings.

Capybeara: "But ... I'm torn, Player V. I know it's safer to have someone by my side, but this whole chaperone business—it makes me feel horribly dependent. And I don't like it. What shall I do?"

What do you say to her?

- A. "You're right. You're an independent, strong girlbear. You don't need a chaperone." (Skip to C-BE)
- B. "Listen to your mom, dear. They know better." (Skip to C-HE)
- C. You sigh. "Truth be told, I don't know ... because I'm scared, too." (Skip to C-RE)

The Endings

C-BE: (Bad Ending): The Vanishing:

You reassure Capybeara of her independence, telling her she doesn't need anyone to watch over her. For a brief moment, her face brightens, but something in her eyes dims—a flicker of uncertainty. Without another word, she turns and walks away, her form blending into the shadows of Thoughtspire.

As she disappears, a quiet emptiness settles over the surroundings, echoing in the silence she leaves behind. You never see her again. Sometimes, in the dead of night, you wonder whether your words sent her deeper into the labyrinth, wandering alone until there was no way back.

> Capybeara, once filled with curiosity and hesitation, has vanished. You're left standing alone in the labyrinth, realizing too late that some choices lead to irreversible paths.

Question: Now that Capybeara is gone, how do you reflect on your choices? Was there a point you could have taken a different turn? How do you reconcile with decisions that lead to lost connections?

    [S/L: Return to Main Menu.]
    C-HE: ("Happy" Ending): The Canary's Song:

You echo her mother's wisdom—*safety first*. Reluctantly, Capybeara agrees, following your guidance like a bird in a gilded cage. Life becomes predictable, shielded from harm, but always confined within the walls of others' expectations. Capybeara is safe, but the vibrant spark of curiosity and defiance that once flickered in her eyes now fades.

Thoughtspire grows quieter around you, its mysteries left unexplored. Perhaps this is what safety feels like: confinement wrapped in a warm blanket of protection. Comfortable, yes, but at the cost of freedom.

> *Capybeara follows the advice of her cautious elders and lives a safe, predictable life—like a canary in a gilded cage. You watch her, content but confined, as the world narrows around her.*

Question: Capybeara is safe, but at what cost? How do you feel about choosing the path of protection over freedom? Was it the right choice, or did it stifle her true potential? What would you have done differently?

    [S/L: Return to Main Menu.]
    C-RE: Real Ending: Walking with Fear

Capybeara watches you closely as you admit the truth—you're scared, too. Fear of the unknown, of failure, of wandering too far from safety without ever making it back. Her eyes soften, as though she's been waiting for those words all along.

    Capybeara: It's not just me then, is it? We all feel this way. Afraid but curious. Dependent but desperate to break free."

    The air shifts. The tension between fear and autonomy thickens, surrounding you both. You're walking a fine line: not fully rejecting the idea of protection, but refusing to let it cage you. You realize now that true autonomy doesn't mean erasing fear—it means acknowledging it without letting it control you.

Lorekeeper: "Perhaps, Player V, it's about understanding that autonomy and caution are not contradictions. Maybe strength is found in acknowledging fear, in balancing protection with the fire that burns within, no?"

The labyrinth seems different now. It's neither fully dangerous nor entirely safe. It reflects something deeper—a fluid core of strength and caution, an understanding that both can coexist without diminishing each other. This is the essence of the Überfrau (Über-Bär?)—fluid, evolving, posthuman.

Capybeara's journey is one of navigating fear and autonomy as intertwined forces. The posthuman subject is not fixed or static (Braidotti, 2013); it embraces vulnerability, acknowledging that fear is part of the human condition, but refusing to let it define or limit the self. The *Überfrau* does not eliminate fear; she transcends it by walking with it, striking a balance between protection and independence. In this moment, you and Capybeara embody this fluidity—the coexistence of autonomy and interdependence, fear and courage, safety and freedom. The labyrinth, too, shifts with you, reflecting the fluid nature of identity, where strength and vulnerability are no longer opposites but companions.

In this real ending, Freud's (1919) theory of the uncanny (*Das Unheimliche*) is particularly apt here—Capybeara's seemingly innocent nature, contrasted with her deep-rooted fears of the "manbear," evokes a strange familiarity that is unsettling. The uncanny arises from something that is both known and alien—Capybeara, though cute and harmless, speaks to the paranoia inherent in every decision about safety and autonomy. What seems familiar and safe (a small, cute bear) becomes tinged with dread, as her speech reveals the existential fear of being prey. This narrative also dives into the theme of "protectionism": choosing safety over independence may keep Capybeara in the "gilded cage" of a controlled life. But how much of her autonomy does she sacrifice to remain safe? The real ending hints at the complex dance between innocence and loss. By acknowledging her fear, she loses some of her innocence but gains a more nuanced understanding of the risks she faces in the labyrinth of Thoughtspire.

Innocence lost and *paranoia* combine to show that protection isn't just about physical safety—it's an emotional and psychological battle between the need for security and the desire for freedom. Capybeara's dilemma is one shared by many: Is it better to live a sheltered, protected life, or embrace the chaos and risk of the unknown? Freud teaches us that what we fear most may come from within—our own instincts to protect ourselves can create the very confinement we seek to escape.

(Capybeara stops in her tracks, listening to your admission of fear. She looks at you with understanding, nodding slightly. In this moment, both of you acknowledge the fluid balance between caution and courage.)

Question: Admitting your own fear has changed the course of the story. How does this acknowledgment shape your understanding of autonomy, safety, and vulnerability? How will you move forward with this newfound awareness of shared fears and insecurities?

[S/L: Return to Main Menu.]

* * *

Shards of You: The Theater of Fractured Selves

The stage is set. A spotlight flickers, revealing fragmented mirrors scattered across the floor. Each shard reflects back distorted versions of you—as well as of Kuromi (Sanrio), Tomie (Junji Ito), and the Lorekeeper (emmmm like I said, your author's, in fact, totally sane). The performance begins, but something is missing ... your voice. You feel like an outsider, watching as they move through their fractured realities.

[Stage Directions]
You find yourself standing in a dimly lit theater—shattered mirrors surround you, reflecting distorted versions of yourself. On stage, the *Lorekeeper*, Kuromi, Tomie, and *you* take your places. The performance is about to begin. But something is off. You feel like you're missing pieces of yourself ... fractured into shards that these strange figures now seem to embody. The *Lorekeeper* steps forward, her voice filled with a sinister glee.

Lorekeeper: "Ah, Player V ... You've made it! Good. You see, we've all been waiting for you. The show can't start without you! Oh, what are these?"

(She gestures toward the blank spaces where fragments of your identity once resided.)

"Tsk. Seems you've left something behind. No matter. We'll help you find yourself again ... piece by piece. Or will we?"

Kuromi: "Don't listen to her, V-chan! She's always losing things. But don't worry, I've got your edge, your sass! But, let's be real, you'll need me to fight through all this fake positivity they keep throwing at you. So much fluff and so little bite."

(She laughs, twirling, a mischievous glint in her eyes.)

Tomie: (Her voice is velvety, seductive, yet terrifyingly cold.) "Oh, Kuromi, darling. You speak too much for someone so small. I am the one you need, Player V. After all, I represent your perfection. Or rather ... your hunger to be perfect. Isn't that why they always come back? Even after they tear me apart, they can't resist putting me back together. You'll learn this too. Everyone will return to you eventually, even if they despise you in the end. The closer you get to them, the more irresistible, yet unbearable, you become. It's a power. Let it consume you."

Lorekeeper: "Oh, and just a quick reminder—No one's getting actually dismembered ... right?"

Cue Player V: _____ (Your line here.)

Lorekeeper: "Oh, don't be shy, Player V. You were always meant to stand here. In this limelight, under the blazing gaze of the world! What's it like, feeling your identity slip through the cracks? Should I tell you, or would you rather find out for yourself?"

Cue Player V: _____ (Your line here.)

Tomie: "Sweet thing, you don't need to be whole. You just need to be ... effective. Sharp. Beautiful in your destruction. Who cares if the pieces fit? We don't exist for 'completeness'—we exist to shatter, to splinter, to leave marks on the world. Isn't that what you want?"

Cue Player V: _____ (Your line here.)

Kuromi: "Why does everyone always try to be so perfect? That's boring, V-chan! Don't you know the fun only starts when things fall apart?"

(She revs her pink and purple chainsaw, sending glitter flying everywhere.)

"We're all just shattered dolls, aren't we? Put together wrong. But that's what makes us interesting. You could try to glue yourself back together, but ... what's the fun in that?"

Tomie: *"Ah, but you do want to be perfect, don't you, Player V? Don't worry, I understand. I too am cursed with this ... allure. They all come back, eventually. Just like you'll keep coming back, craving their approval even as you crumble beneath it."*

Cue Player V: _____ (Your line here.)

Lorekeeper: *"Player V, you don't find yourself in Thoughtspire. You* create *yourself. Each shard you pick up is a choice—a new version of you. So why be the same as before? The shards aren't pieces of some puzzle to solve. Are you afraid of that?"*

(She pauses for a moment, considering, before adding:)

"It's like what my 8-year-old roommate said once—if you tear apart a Lego figure and reassemble it, piece by piece, is it still the same figure? Is it still Bob? Or is it something entirely new, just using Bob's parts? If identity is tied to continuity of consciousness, rather than the material pieces, then does it matter what the pieces are made of (Locke, 1975)? It's the same with you, Player V. Your identity isn't fixed in those shards—it's fluid, created by your choices."

Kuromi: *"Ah, so we're pulling a Locke now, are we? Identity as a stream of consciousness. But what about Heraclitus? You know, the guy who said you can't step into the same river twice (Heraclitus, 2001)? If you're always changing, can you ever be 'you' again after you've torn yourself apart and reassembled? Do you even want to be?"*

Tomie: *"Reassembly is the fun part. It's when you decide what pieces stay and what pieces* get left behind. *If Bob isn't Bob anymore, who cares? You'll be 'better' than Bob. Who needs the old version anyway?"*

Lorekeeper: *"If you tear yourself apart and reassemble ... Locke would argue that as long as your consciousness continues, you're still you. But Heraclitus would say you've become something else. And isn't that the point? The uncertainties. The paradox. The constant suffering."*

Cue Player V: _____ (Your line here.)

Kuromi: *"Afraid? Pshh. Come on, Player V. Fear is for people who haven't figured it out yet. It's not about putting the pieces back. It's about what you do with them, no?"*

(Her voice takes on a teasing edge, as she twirls again, dangerously close to the mirror shards on the floor.)

"Careful, though ... pick the wrong piece, and you might cut *yourself."*

Tomie: *"The fun part is ... you never know which shard will cut the deepest. Maybe it'll be one from the past. Maybe from something you haven't even lived yet. Isn't that the thrill of it all? Finding out which piece hurts the most."*

Lorekeeper: "Player V, are you still looking for the 'right' piece? How quaint. You'll never know which version of you is the right one. And that's fine. Wholeness is an illusion. Perfection is just a lie people tell themselves to keep from facing the truth. But here, in Thoughtspire, we face the truth every day."

Cue Player V: _____ (Your line here.)

Kuromi: "Come on, don't be boring. Let's see what you become."

Tomie: "Or walk away. Stay the same."
(Her smile fades, replaced by cold indifference.)
The choice is yours.

Kuromi: "Tick-tock, Player V. Time's running out."

Tomie, "And remember, we'll be watching … "

[Ending the Scene]

The lights dim, and the fragmented mirrors reflect only pieces of Kuromi, Tomie, and the Lorekeeper. Each one is a distorted shard, a version of them—and maybe a version of you. The stage grows silent as they wait for your next move.

Modern identity, as shaped by the relentless scrutiny of the public gaze, exists in a state of fragmentation—caught between visibility and vulnerability, desire and despise. In Lacanian terms, the mirror stage represents the moment when the self perceives itself as an object, a coherent whole, through the reflection in the mirror. However, this wholeness is always illusory, masking the fragmented nature of the individual beneath the surface (Lacan, 1982). As Player V navigates Thoughtspire, the fractured mirrors reflect the multiplicity of identities—each one a shard of what we present to others and what we hide from them.

And it's finally the right time to disclose the real research question behind this hauntingly absurd gameplay setting:

How does StrataPlay facilitate the exploration of "Strata" narratives, supporting individual interpretations of the *Überfrau* as a fluid, evolving status rather than a fixed ideal?

Ah, Player V, you have wandered far and wide through Thoughtspire's labyrinth, twisting through its hallways of absurdity, haunted mirrors, and fractured selves. And as you stand here at the final threshold, isn't it clear? The Überfrau—like you, like me—isn't a finished product, nor a single mold to fill. She's an idea, a process, a shifting, evolving state of being that escapes easy definition.

StrataPlay tells stories, holding space for stories to tell themselves, to be rewritten, remixed, and reinterpreted—each layer of narrative offering another path, another reflection of self. We've moved through *chaos*, through *absurdity*, and even through *haunting familiarity*. But the power here, Player V, is in seeing yourself mirrored, fragmented, and continually reassembled—not into a singular, "superhuman" identity—but into something infinitely more complex, more fluid, more real.

The *Überfrau* isn't a lofty ideal you either achieve or fail. No, she is *you in motion*. She is the tension between visibility and vulnerability, desire and despise, conformity and autonomy. She is both *player* and *prey*. And perhaps the real challenge is this: how do we live with the contradictions?

So here we are, dear Player V. Maybe you've figured it out, or maybe you're still chasing answers through the maze. Either way, you've played your part in the game of StrataPlay, where the pieces shift, identities splinter, and the *Überfrau* dances between the cracks of the mirror.

Now, it's time to leave Thoughtspire ... or not. Perhaps you'll linger a little longer, contemplate the shards that still glint at your feet.

The choice, as always, is yours.

GG

Dumb Ways to Die as a Lorekeeper

So here we are—starting a chapter and closing out a book that I've poured my heart, soul, and questionable sanity into, with a title that begins with "GG." Not exactly the most promising move, is it?

For those of you who've already forgotten the cheeky little safeword system we established, *GG* stands for *Good Game*—that moment in gaming where you throw in the towel, wave the white flag, and admit you're ready to give up (usually with a mix of grace and frustration, depending on how epic the defeat). But in the spirit of keeping things fun—and because I just like how it looks—we're sticking with it as the title for this not-so-grand finale.

And if you recall from *Game Start* way back in Chapter 2, I did promise the grand premiere of the ultimate anthem for lorekeepers. So, without further ado, here it is: *Dumb Ways to Die as a Lorekeeper*, performed by none other than New StrataPlay—the K-Pop group you never saw coming.

#Dumb Ways to Die as a Lorekeeper

> *Performed by New StrataPlay*
> Produced by: The Lorekeeper Collective™
> Executive Producer: Überfrau Entertainment
> Mixed & Mastered at Thoughtspire Studios
> Special Guest Appearances: Kuromi, Tomie, and Player V
> Genre: *Absurdity Pop*

Drowning in infinite footnotes,
Eaten by a peer-reviewed beast,
Forgot to use a safeword,
And now I'm truly deceased.

Falling into the posthuman abyss,
Thinking this was a quant study—what a miss,
Over-interpreting everything,
While the narrative's supposed to sing.

[Chorus]
Dumb ways to die, so many dumb ways to die,
Dumb ways to die as a Lorekeeper in Thoughtspire.

Forgot I'm the Lorekeeper in this maze,
Daydreaming about dismembering players,
Turned into a dung beetle, what a fall,
Posthumanism consumed me, after all.

Spent all my money on Kuromi toys,
Stuck in Thoughtspire, losing my poise,
Playing StrataPlay till I'm fried,
I guess this is how I've died.

[Chorus]
Dumb ways to die, so many dumb ways to die,
Dumb ways to die as a Lorekeeper in Thoughtspire.

Giggling at my game design all day,
Fell for Gojo Satoru in a tragic way,
Overwhelmed by marginalia, so dense,
Caught in a feedback loop that makes no sense.

Trapped in a Zoom call, it won't end,
Lost in a maze of rooms—help, my friend!
Can't stop writing haiku, just for fun,
Started talking like Gen Alpha—what have I done?

[Chorus]
Dumb ways to die, so many dumb ways to die,
Dumb ways to die as a Lorekeeper in Thoughtspire.

Staring contest with a frog, I can't break,
Throwing paperwork at the gatekeeper—my mistake!
Begging Player V, "please come back,"
Rewriting syllabi that nobody'll track.

Accidentally summoned Confucius,
Who now lectures me on virtue and justice,
Turned into a sentient citation, what a mess,
Crushed by books I never read, I confess.

[Chorus]
Dumb ways to die, so many dumb ways to die,
Dumb ways to die as a Lorekeeper in Thoughtspire.

Forgot the research question, oh no,
Now I'm stuck in academic limbo,
Lorekeeper's lost to absurdity's call,
And that's how I've met my dumbest fall.

[Chorus]
Dumb ways to die, so many dumb ways to die,
Dumb ways to die as a Lorekeeper in Thoughtspire.

GG, Players. What a wild ride it's been.

You've navigated Thoughtspire, embraced the absurdity, danced with chaos, and maybe even survived a few dumb ways to die. But as with all great games, it's time to log off ... for now.

Until the next level, dear players—

Stay sharp, stay fluid, and remember: *the Lorekeeper's always watching.*

Press any key to continue:
[Resume Y/N]
[Return to Main Menu]

Bibliography

Abraham, N., & Torok, M. (1994). *The shell and the kernel: Renewals of psychoanalysis.* University of Chicago Press.
Abram, D. (1996). *The Spell of the Sensuous: Perception and Language in a More-Than-Human World.* Vintage.
Ahmed, S. (2004). *The cultural politics of emotion.* Routledge.
Bachelard, G. (1964). *The poetics of space.* Beacon Press.
Ball, S. J. (2016). Neoliberal education? Confronting the slouching beast. *Policy Futures in Education, 14*(8), 1046–1059. <https://doi.org/10.1177/1478210316664259>
Barad, K. (2007). *Meeting the universe halfway: Quantum physics and the entanglement of matter and meaning.* Duke University Press.
Barthes, R. (1977). *Image-Music-Text.* Hill and Wang.
Baudrillard, J. (1983). *Simulacra and Simulation.* University of Michigan Press.
Beauvoir, S. de. (1947). *The Ethics of Ambiguity.* Philosophical Library.
Beckett, S. (1953). *Waiting for Godot.* Grove Press.
Bergson, H. (1907). *Creative Evolution.* Henry Holt and Company.
Braidotti, R. (1994). *Nomadic subjects: Embodiment and sexual difference in contemporary feminist theory.* Columbia University Press.
Braidotti, R. (2013). *The Posthuman.* Polity Press.
Braidotti, R. (2017). *Posthuman, All Too Human: The Tanner Lectures on Human Values.* Yale University.
Brown, P. C., Roediger, H. L., & McDaniel, M. A. (2014). *Make it stick: The science of successful learning.* Harvard University Press.

Butler, J. (1990). *Gender Trouble*. Routledge
Cai, Z. (2013). *How to Read Chinese Poetry: A Guided Anthology*. Columbia University Press.
Camus, A. (1942). *The Myth of Sisyphus*. Gallimard.
Carel, H. (2016). *Phenomenology of Illness*. Oxford University Press.
Caruth, C. (1996). *Unclaimed experience: Trauma, narrative, and history*. Johns Hopkins University Press.
Cheng, A. A. (2001). *The melancholy of race: Psychoanalysis, assimilation, and hidden grief*. Oxford University Press.
Cooper, J. M. (1999). *Reason and emotion: Essays on Ancient Moral Psychology and Ethical Theory*. Princeton University Press.
Cytowic, R. E. (2002). *Synesthesia: A union of the senses* (2nd ed.). MIT Press.
Davis, L. J. (1995). *Enforcing Normalcy: Disability, Deafness, and the Body*. Verso.
Deleuze, G., & Guattari, F. (1987). *A Thousand Plateaus: Capitalism and Schizophrenia*. University of Minnesota Press.
Derrida, J. (1967). *Of Grammatology*. Johns Hopkins University Press.
Elbow, P. (1973). *Writing Without Teachers*. Oxford University Press.
Emerson, B. (2019). *The public's law: Origins and architecture of progressive democracy*. Oxford University Press.
Erickson, F. (2018). *The Challenge of Teaching*. Harvard University Press.
Ericsson, K. A., Krampe, R. T., & Tesch-Römer, C. (1993). The role of deliberate practice in the acquisition of expert performance. *Psychological Review, 100*(3), 363–406.
Faris, W. B. (2004). *Ordinary Enchantments: Magical Realism and the Remystification of Narrative*. Vanderbilt University Press.
Foucault, M. (1977). *Discipline and punish: The birth of the prison*. Pantheon Books.
Foucault, M. (1988). *Technologies of the Self*. University of Massachusetts Press.
Frankl, V. E. (1984). *Man's Search for Meaning*. Beacon Press.
Freud, S. (1919). The Uncanny. In J. Strachey (Ed.), *The Standard Edition of the Complete Psychological Works of Sigmund Freud* (Vol. XVII, pp. 217–256). Hogarth Press.
Gallagher, S. (2017). *Enactivist Interventions: Rethinking the Mind*. Oxford University Press.
Garland-Thomson, R. (2011). Misfits: A Feminist Materialist Disability Concept. *Hypatia, 26*(3), 591–609.
Gergen, K. J. (1991). *The saturated self: Dilemmas of identity in contemporary life*. Basic Books.
Giroux, H. A. (2011). *On Critical Pedagogy*. Bloomsbury.
Gray, J., O'Regan, J. P., & Wallace, C. (2018). Education and the discourse of global neo-liberalism. *Language and Intercultural Communication, 18*(5), 471–477. <https://doi.org/10.1080/14708477.2018.1501842>
Haraway, D. (1991). *Simians, cyborgs, and women: The reinvention of nature*. Routledge.
Haraway, D. (2016). *Staying with the Trouble: Making Kin in the Chthulucene*. Duke University Press.
He, M. (2003). *Cultural reconciliation and narrative transformation*. Peter Lang.

Hegel, G. W. F. (1977). *Phenomenology of Spirit* (A. V. Miller, Trans.). Oxford University Press. (Original work published 1807).
Heidegger, M. (1927). *Being and Time*. Harper Perennial Modern Classics.
Heraclitus. (2001). *Fragments* (T. M. Robinson, Trans.). University of Toronto Press. (Original work published c. 500 B.C.E.)
Hirsch, M. (1997). *Family frames: Photography, narrative, and postmemory*. Harvard University Press.
Huizinga, J. (1949). *Homo Ludens: A Study of the Play-Element in Culture*. Routledge & Kegan Paul.
Ingleby, E. (2021). *Neoliberalism Across Education*. Springer International Publishing.
Kaltenmark, M. (1969). *Lao Tzu and Taoism*. Stanford University Press.
Korsmeyer, C. (1999). *Making sense of taste: Food and philosophy*. Cornell University Press.
Kristeva, J. (1980). *Powers of Horror: An Essay on Abjection*. Columbia University Press.
Lacan, J. (1982). *Écrits: A selection* (A. Sheridan, Trans.). Norton & Company.
Laozi. (300 BCE). *Tao Te Ching*. Translated by D. C. Lau, Penguin Classics, 1963.
Lather, P. (2013). Methodology-21: What do we do in the afterward? *International Journal of Qualitative Studies in Education, 26*(6), 634–645.
Linehan, M. M. (1993). *Skills Training Manual for Treating Borderline Personality Disorder*. Guilford Press.
Linton, S. (1998). *Claiming Disability: Knowledge and Identity*. New York University Press.
Locke, J. (1975). *An essay concerning human understanding* (P. H. Nidditch, Ed.). Oxford University Press. (Original work published 1690)
McAdams, D. P. (2001). The Psychology of Life Stories. *Review of General Psychology, 5*(2), 100–122.
Mead, G. H. (1934). *Mind, self, and society*. University of Chicago Press.
Merleau-Ponty, M. (1962). *Phenomenology of Perception*. Routledge & Kegan Paul.
Mignolo, W. (2011). *The Darker Side of Western Modernity: Global Futures, Decolonial Options*. Duke University Press.
Nietzsche, F. (1974). *The gay science* (W. Kaufmann, Trans.). Vintage Books. (Original work published 1882)
Nietzsche, F. (1998). *Beyond good and evil*. Dover Publications.
Nietzsche, F. (2006). *Thus spoke Zarathustra* (A. Del Caro & R. Pippin, Trans.). Cambridge University Press. (Original work published 1883)
Piaget, J. (1962). *Play, dreams and imitation in childhood*. Norton.
Pinar, W. F. (2006). *The Synoptic Text Today and Other Essays: Curriculum Development After the Reconceptualization*. Peter Lang.
Pinar, W. F. (2023). *Awakenings to the calling of nonviolence in curriculum studies*. Peter Lang.
Rich, A. (1986). *Of woman born: Motherhood as experience and institution*. W. W. Norton & Company.
Ricoeur, P. (1992). *Oneself as Another*. University of Chicago Press.
Rogers, C. R. (1961). *On Becoming a Person: A Therapist's View of Psychotherapy*. Houghton Mifflin.

Rosiek, J. (2024, September 2). Re-turning: A Review of Posthumanist Educational Research. [Video]. *Postqualitative research.* YouTube. <https://www.youtube.com/watch?v=Pv07l4Wr9mw>

Rostand, E. (1897). *Cyrano de Bergerac: Heroic comedy in five acts* (B. Hooker, Trans.). Bantam Classics. (Original work published 1897)

Ruddick, S. (1989). *Maternal thinking: Toward a politics of peace.* Beacon Press.

Said, E. W. (1978). *Orientalism.* Pantheon Books.

Sartre, J. P. (1993). *Being and Nothingness.* Washington Square.

Savage, G. (2017). Neoliberalism, education and curriculum. In B. Lingard, G. Thompson, & S. Sellar (Eds.), *Powers of Curriculum: Sociological Perspectives on Education* (pp. 143–165). Oxford University Press.

Snaza, N. (2024). *Tendings: Feminist Esoterisms and the Abolition of Man.* Duke University Press.

Sontag, S. (1964). *Against Interpretation and Other Essays.* Farrar, Straus & Giroux.

Spivak, G. C. (1999). *A Critique of Postcolonial Reason: Toward a History of the Vanishing Present.* Harvard University Press.

St. Pierre, E. A. (2011). Post-qualitative research: The critique and the coming after. In N. K. Denzin & Y. S. Lincoln (Eds.), *The SAGE handbook of qualitative research* (4th ed., pp. 611–625). Sage Publications.

St. Pierre, E. A. (2013). The posts continue: becoming. *International Journal of Qualitative Studies in Education, 26*(6), 646–657. <https://doi.org/10.1080/09518398.2013.788754>

St. Pierre, E. A. (2016). Rethinking the Empirical in the Posthuman. In: Taylor, C. A., Hughes, C. (eds) *Posthuman Research Practices in Education.* Palgrave Macmillan, London. <https://doi.org/10.1057/9781137453082_3>

Toffler, A. (1970). *Future Shock.* Random House.

Turkle, S. (1995). *Life on the screen: Identity in the age of the internet.* Simon & Schuster.

Vygotsky, L. S. (1978). *Mind in society: The development of higher psychological processes.* Harvard University Press.

Wang, H. (2004). *The Call from the Stranger on a Journey Home: Curriculum in a Third Space.* Peter Lang Publishing.

Wang, H. (2010). A zero space of nonviolence. *Journal of Curriculum Theorizing, 26*(1), 1–8.

Wang, H. (2013). A nonviolent approach to social justice education. *Educational Studies, 49*(6), 485–503.

Ward, J. (2013). Synesthesia. *Annual Review of Psychology, 64*, 49–75. <https://doi.org/10.1146/annurev-psych-113011-1-143840>

Williams, P. (1989). *Mahayana Buddhism: The Doctrinal Foundations.* Routledge.

Winnicott, D. W. (1971). *Playing and Reality.* Tavistock Publications.

Index

A

A Prey in Thoughtspire, 76
abjection, 15
Absurdism, 45
Aristotle, 4

B

Basho-san. *See* Matsuo Bashō
Bashō-san, 72

C

Camus, 7
Capybeara, 71, 78
CD. *See* StrataPlay Safeword System
Chthulucene. *See* Posthumanism
Contours of Cacophony, 24
Contours of Silence, 21
Critical Romance Theory. *See* CRT
CRT, 52

cultural analogies, 57
cyborg, 3
Cyrano, 7, 22

D

debate, 4
dialectic, 4, 6
différance, 22
Doraemon, 22

E

endarkenment, 8
endarkenness, 75
Escapism, 10

F

first-person shooter (FPS), 59
Folklore Mashup™, 18, 60
Future Shock, 6

G

Gen Alpha, 18, 20, 48
GG, 69, 86, *See* StrataPlay Safeword System

H

haiku, 4, 72
Hunter x Hunter, 71
Hyperreality, 44

I

Index Cards, 27, 60
Infinite Void, 6, 23
intra-action, 13

J

Jujutsu Kaisen, 6
Junji Ito, 7

K

kawaii, 8, 49
K-Pop, 18, 64, 65
Kuromi, 19, 36, 47, 81

L

Laozi, 5, 22
Liang Shanbo and Zhu Yingtai, 56
Little Red, 71, 76
lived experience, 24
Lorekeeper, 11, 13, 19, 42

M

Magical-Post-Realism, 17, 44
making kin, 5
Maternal Thinking, 32
Matsuo Bashō, 4
Multiplicity, 13

N

Narrative Identity Theory, 24
Neal Libertas, 17, 47
New StrataPlay, 65
nonviolence, 8
nothingness, 6
NPC, 3

O

OT. *See* StrataPlay Safeword System

P

panopticism, 15
peace, 8
player, 13
Player V, 82
Poetic Translation Fail™, 18, 66
Post-Edu Apocalypse, 17, 45
Posthumanism, 5, 13, 45, 56
postmemory, 17, 31
Post-Presence Epoch, 7
postqualitative, 31, 41, 56
Postqualitative Inquiry, 12
PQI. *See* Postqualitative Inquiry

R

RPG, 3, 17, 44

S

Sanrio, 7
Shards of You, 72, 81
Sisyphus, 7
StrataPlay, 9, 12, 13, 20, 84
StrataPlay Safeword System, 69
Stream of Consciousness, 74
Synesthesia, 16, 21, 26

T

Tao Te Ching, 5
The Analects, 56
The Masquerade of Validation, 71, 72
The Ultimate X Collab™, 18, 56
Thoughtspire, 17, 74, 89
Tomie, 7, 19, 74, 81
tragic optimism, 24
trauma, 31

U

Überfrau, 14, 19, 84
Überfrau Manifesto, 69

V

Valorant, 59

W

wúxíng, 22

Ludic Scholarship
Games, Learning and Innovative Pedagogy

This series focuses on the intersection of gamification, ludology, pedagogy, and innovative methodological thinking, offering a space for cutting-edge scholarship that bridges game-based approaches with educational theory and practice. Ludic Scholarship highlights gamified learning and emergent methodologies that challenge traditional research frameworks, encouraging transformative approaches to teaching, learning, meaning-making, and the construction of knowledge.

The series invites contributions that explore how game mechanics, narrative structures, and immersive environments are reshaping learning practices across disciplines. From theoretical explorations of ludic strategies to applied case studies of gamified pedagogy, Ludic Scholarship emphasizes creativity and academic rigor, inviting works that challenge established conventions. Targeting educators, researchers, and curriculum scholars, this series supports interdisciplinary collaborations and post-qualitative approaches that investigate the dynamic role of games and play in 21st-century education.

Editorial Address:
Dr. Mila Zhu
Southeastern Oklahoma State University,
Educational Instruction & Leadership
E-mail: mzhu@se.edu

Vol. 1   Johnathan deHaan & James York Freedom to Play. A Ludic Language Pedagogy Primer. 600 pages. 2025. ISBN 9781636675961

Vol. 2   Dr. Mila Zhu. The StrataPlay Methodology. A Lorekeeper's Game Design in Postqualitative Inquiry. c. 144 pages. 2025. ISBN 9783034354837

www.ingramcontent.com/pod-product-compliance
Lightning Source LLC
Chambersburg PA
CBHW052025290426
44112CB00014B/2383